HAPPILY EVER AFTER

*8 Principles for
Healing a Broken Heart*

T0163746

SUKI SOHN

NEW YORK

LONDON • NASHVILLE • MELBOURNE • VANCOUVER

Happily Ever After

8 Principles for Healing a Broken Heart

Published in New York, New York, by Morgan James Publishing in partnership with Difference Press. Morgan James is a trademark of Morgan James, LLC. www.MorganJamesPublishing.com

The Morgan James Speakers Group can bring authors to your live event. For more information or to book an event visit The Morgan James Speakers Group at www.TheMorganJamesSpeakersGroup.com.

ISBN 9781683508281 paperback
ISBN 9781683508298 eBook
Library of Congress Control Number: 2017917158

Cover Design by:
Megan Whitney
megan@creativeninjadesigns.com

Interior Design by:
Chris Treccani
www.3dogcreative.net

In an effort to support local communities, raise awareness and funds, Morgan James Publishing donates a percentage of all book sales for the life of each book to Habitat for Humanity Peninsula and Greater Williamsburg.

Get involved today! Visit
www.MorganJamesBuilds.com

Happily Ever After

DEDICATION

For all the brave souls who ardently seek True Love.

You are forever pure,
You are forever true
And the dream of this world can never touch you
So give up your attachments
Give up your confusion
And fly to that space that is beyond all illusion

Suddhossi buddhossi niranjanosi
Samsara maya parivar jitosi
Samsara svapanam
Traija mohan nidram
Na janma mrityor
Tat sat sva rupee

from a Vedic Lullaby Suddhosi Buddhosi
as Translated by Shimshai

TABLE OF CONTENTS

PREFACE

I did not set out to become an intuitive healer or guide for women to find love. In fact, I initially followed a more predictable path: a corporate job with an MBA and a marriage to a promising young banker. The dissolution of my marriage was also the dissolution of my identity as I knew it. Things that I held significant and meaningful were no longer important to me. Instead, there was a big gaping hole in my life.

For the following decade, I studied many different esoteric spiritual paths to fill this hole and find purpose and direction in my life again. I have learned that across all ancient esoteric traditions, there are some shared core beliefs regarding human experience in this world. These are:

- Everything is alive and has a life force.
- The physical realm is only a small spectrum of "reality" but most real to humans due to the limitations of our five senses.
- Awareness and validation of the metaphysical realm is the first step towards unlocking the secrets of this world.

- Everything and everyone is our teacher. We may choose to hurt from our experiences or learn from them.
- Compassion and a deep union with nature allow us to see and live from the eyes of our heart. The practice of living in this manner brings illumination to all aspects of life.
- There is a divine purpose for all things.
- Everyone has the birth right and ability to directly communicate with the metaphysical realms.

Despite some differences, all ancient traditions are consistent in the intention of weaving reverence and expanded awareness into the ordinary ways of life to bring forth healing and wholeness. These core beliefs are the foundation for the MAGNETIC Process outlined in this book. By connecting to Spirit and increasing self-awareness with time, practice, and study, we will be able to shift patterns in our psyche and release old wounds and traumas held within. When we mend our hearts and become whole again, we are naturally MAGNETIC and thus, the love we dream of becomes inevitable.

I do not have a PhD in psychology or neuroscience. However, what I do have is a first-hand experience of what you are going through – the doubt, fear and perhaps even cynicism about romantic love. My deepest desire is to be of assistance to you in your path towards true love and devotion to your true self

Suki Sohn
June 1, 2017
Irvington, NY

CHAPTER 1

Why Don't You Have the Relationship of Your Dreams?

The kids are in bed now. It's been a long day. Things have been stressful at work and for the second time this week, Jackie has been contacted by the school regarding her son's unruly behavior. He is a good kid and rationally she knows things will get better, but she can't help but feel exhausted and alone, very alone in the world. Nursing a glass of wine, she mindlessly watches TV so that she can shut down the constant churning of her mind. She eventually turns the light off and lies in bed staring at the ceiling, when suddenly she is overcome by the overwhelming feeling of loneliness. She reasons with herself that things could be worse, but at the moment she feels utterly alone. She curls up into a fetal position and quietly starts to cry. She feels a deep cutting pain in her heart reminiscing on the memories of betrayal and mourns how jaded she became about romance and love. Yet she still longs to feel the comfort of a pair of strong arms wrapped around her to make everything right again.

It has been three years since her messy divorce. She has been on many dates and even had some short-lived relationships, but now she wonders if she will ever find love again. She got married in her early twenties and after fifteen years, her marriage dissolved painfully. Now in her late thirties, she feels like a fish out of water when it comes to dating. She finds the numerous dating apps intimidating and distasteful at the same time.

Maria, on the other hand, is a man eater. She's a voluptuous woman with a hearty appetite for sex. A true feminist, she outwardly revels in the plethora of options available to her through dating apps. She keeps her romantic dalliances carefully separate from her role as a mother. In a way, this suits her. She can dedicate herself to her children most of the time, while finding excitement with her various lovers. She does not allow herself to get emotionally attached, or so she thinks. Despite the attention from her string of lovers, in her most vulnerable moments, she finds herself in tears with a deep longing in her heart for a more meaningful relationship.

Does either Jackie's or Maria's story strike a chord with you? Does it seem like you've got everything else under control, but romance is the one area in your life you just can't get a handle on? Have you had a streak of bad luck with men? Maybe you've now convinced yourself that you don't need a man in your life, and perhaps you are better off without one. Romantic love just doesn't seem to be worth the heartache and trouble. With your career and kids, perhaps life seems full enough. Are you just too tired and exhausted of being all things to all people that you can't muster up the energy to contemplate going on a date? Or perhaps it's been such a long while since you've been on a date that the whole idea of dating is plain intimidating. With the overabundance of dating apps, does the idea of swiping to find your match make you cringe?

Yet, you know that in your heart of hearts, you ache for the hopeful little girl who once dreamt of falling in love and living happily ever after.

What is it costing you to not have a partner with whom you can share life's ups and downs? Beyond the obvious emotional support we receive from our relationships, we are biologically designed for intimate physical contact. A simple hug releases positive brain chemicals like endorphin, dopamine, and serotonin, which are crucial to our emotional well-being. Intimate contact also lowers blood pressure, supports a healthy heart, and boosts our immune system. Women, whose brains are wired for collaboration and physical contact, suffer more acutely from the lack of intimate touch. As such, insomnia, anxiety, depression, and many nervous disorders are common among professional women (and especially single working moms) who lack an intimate and loving relationship in their lives.

Jackie, after several years of dating mishaps, finally did find her way to Mark, a wonderfully loving and supportive man. They are now happily married with another child of their own on the way. Her relationship with Mark is a transformative one that brought so much more than romance into her life. Jackie finally found the love she desired because she was able to get past her old stories about men and face her own inner demons that prevented her from freely receiving and giving love. Maria was also able to find a committed long-term relationship when she finally realized that her beliefs around men were her defense mechanism to avoid getting hurt again.

At this point, you may be thinking that stories like this apply to others, but not you. You may believe stories like, "all the good men are taken," "all men cheat," or, "I'm just not one of the lucky ones." Perhaps you feel like your best days are behind you and have simply resigned yourself to accepting a life without ever being cherished or loved by a man.

Love is truly all around us. You can have the romantic relationship of your dreams if you truly and daringly choose it. This will require taking a hard look at some of your preconceptions, beliefs and upgrading your understanding of love, men, and relationships. Relationships shape who we are, and of the many relationships we have, romantic love is the most intimate and revealing of them all. There is nowhere to hide in a committed long-term relationship, and because of this, it's the most continuously challenging relationship to nurture.

I am not claiming that the journey to true love is an easy one, but I can offer some guidance to help you identify and avoid some of the common pitfalls. I have first-hand witnessed and experienced some of the Band-Aid solutions out there that offer advice on how to land the man of your dreams. In many ways, it is this attitude towards relationships that is at the very core of the problem. Your lover is not a trophy to be won nor the solution to all of life's problems. A successful relationship requires sincerity, a genuine respect for one another, and most of all, committed effort.

I do not offer cheap parlor tricks or superficial advice to make you temporarily attractive to a man. Drawing upon ancient wisdom and modern scientific discoveries, my aim is to help you to access and uncover the unique beauty you possess so that you can naturally attract the relationship you deserve.

In this book, I will introduce eight basic principles to attract and nurture a long-term romantic relationship, which I call the MAGNETIC Process. But before I share my insights that I have discovered along the way, I would like to share my journey that brought me to where I am now.

CHAPTER 2
My Love Story

"The minute I heard my first love story
I started looking for you,
not knowing how blind that was.
Lovers don't finally meet somewhere.
They're in each other all along."
-Rumi

The Banker

My first husband was a banker. He was a handsome Eurasian man from Oxford. Not only was he well-educated and worldly, he was 6'3", and had mysterious green-grey eyes and a six-pack that even a professional athlete would envy. Never emotional and always cool as a cucumber, he checked off everything on my Mr. Right list. And he adored me. What more could a girl ask for?

During my time with my Banker, my passions were around my career and financial success. To me, life was a check-list. I was at the time an up-and-coming executive at the Walt Disney Company. I guess we were what they call a power couple. My wardrobe was filled with designer clothing, we traveled to exotic locations, and stayed at six-star hotels. We had a 4,000-square-foot condo overlooking beautiful Hong Kong Harbor, and to top it all off, I had just given birth to a healthy baby boy.

On the surface, my life seemed charmed. But one fateful day, all that fell apart. My Banker and I had just gotten back from a safari trip to Kenya. On the first day back in my office, as I was going through voicemails, I came across a strange message from a woman saying that she had been having an affair with my husband for the past year and a half. I was so incredulous that I was about to hit delete, thinking that she got the wrong number. Then she started talking about details of my life that made me realize she was talking about me! I felt the blood in my veins run cold and ran out of the office crying.

How could I have been so clueless? My husband and I had not been having that much sex at the time. In fact, getting pregnant with my first son almost seemed like immaculate conception. But for a year and a half?

Everything that seemed so important suddenly didn't matter to me anymore – the job, the money, the apartment – it all seemed hollow. I used to think that if I was perfect, I would be loved. I was immaculately groomed and was an upcoming hot shot at work. How could any man not love me?

My baby boy was only nine months old. I had to try to make things work somehow. I spent the next nine months trying to make sense of things and keep the marriage together. I smoked a pack of cigarettes every day, and spent most of my non-working hours locked in my room, depressed. Almost eight months passed like this, when I received another phone call that shattered my life completely. My best friend called me to tell me that she just found out that my Banker had never stopped seeing this other woman. That was it. I realized it was time to go.

I quit my job, packed my bags, and moved to New York City. And promptly and quite unexpectedly fell in love with another man.

The Chef

I meant him to be my rebound guy. He was a chef. A sensuous, tall, dark, and handsome Italian guy, oozing with sex appeal. (Ok, I admit. I read one too many steamy romance novels as a teen, and developed a rather misguided weakness for the tall, dark, and handsome type.)

With my Chef, the passions of my five senses were ignited. Until I met my Chef, I had no idea that I had completely shut down the sensual side of me. I was too preoccupied with my check list that I had not stopped to feel pleasure. Really feel pleasure. And oh man, did it feel good…

The sex was amazing. The kind of sex that warms your body and make your knees go weak just thinking about it. My life was filled with sensual experiences in and out of the bedroom. And in some way I felt that I deserved it after the emotional desert that was my marriage for so many years.

With my Chef, I visited many Michelin-star restaurants around the world and had some amazing and exotic experiences. Debauched parties to exotic meals after hours where species close to extinction were on the menu. With him I tasted the sweetness of the forbidden apple in more ways than I care to remember. Then I got pregnant.

We were madly in love and our families were blending nicely, so we thought we'd try to make it work. Until his kids found out that I was pregnant. They went berserk, and my Chef fell apart. He was already wrestling with the guilt of leaving his children as his father had left him when he was young. Four months into my pregnancy, I couldn't take it anymore. I decided to terminate the pregnancy. I didn't want to be a single mom with *two* young toddlers. I didn't have the courage to do that.

As I lay down on the cold clinical bed with legs spread by stirrups, I cried and cried. The nurse with her latex-gloved hands wiped my tears and said to me, "Don't do this to yourself." I couldn't stop crying… I was tormented. Having known what it's like to feel life growing inside me and having already felt the feathering touches of the baby inside me, I was devastated. My soul was ripped apart. Blood was on my hands. I felt like I murdered my own child. I could not forgive the Chef for not making me feel safe enough to keep this baby. But more so, I could not forgive myself for going through with it. I had nightmares about it for years after.

Needless to say, my relationship with my Chef started crumbling from there. Our relationship was built on sensuality and pleasure, and I could no longer feel any of it. The final nail in the coffin was, again, a phone call. This time from my cousin, who told me that she had just had lunch with a woman who claimed to be my Chef's girlfriend.

At this point, I made the conclusion that all men cheat and cannot be trusted.

I felt such passion and deep emotions with my Chef. I felt that he was my soulmate, the love of my life. Now what? What is love? What really is the purpose life? I went through a period of deep soul searching. Years passed without a significant relationship. I felt too wounded to try.

The Healer

I was desperately seeking something to give meaning to my heartbreak. I studied many esoteric spiritual traditions including Kabbalah, Vipassana meditation, ThetaHealing®, and Tibetan Bon Shamanic traditions. I also become a master in Feng Shui, Tai Chi, and Qigong.

It was during this time I met my Healer. He and I were friends for a few years before we got romantically involved. Through patience and kindness, he slowly soothed my wounds and opened my heart. I dare say for the first time. I learned to love and accept myself with no pre-condition of being a successful career woman or a sexy lover.

He was not like other men I dated. Though I found him physically attractive, he didn't go to the right schools, he wasn't financially stable, and he was much too bohemian for me. Two weeks into "dating" him, I broke up with him saying that the relationship simply could not work long term and that I wasn't interested in a fling. But I missed his friendship. I had other men pursuing me at the time, so I realized he was more than just filling an empty space. He didn't say much when I reached out to him but sent me a song that expressed how he felt. The song was called *Song to the Siren* by This Mortal Coil. The haunting sound and lyrics touched my heart.

He was not afraid to be vulnerable in front of me. There was no bravado in his attitude and he never tried to hide how he was hurt by my actions. During the time of my inner turmoil of accepting him as my man, he simply said to me, "women are like the moon and tides. They change. I accept you as you are with all your changes, but *I* am not going anywhere." Those were the sexiest words anyone could say to me.

I knew that I wanted to be with him but I also knew that he needed to step up his game in order for the relationship to work. I very bluntly told him so. Dating is different and more complicated when you are a single mom and floating along with his bohemian and carefree lifestyle wasn't going to work for me. He agreed not just in words but with his actions.

18 months later he became my life companion and the father to my second son.

The Snake, the Jaguar, the Humming Bird and the Eagle

Quero shamans of Peru say that humans can operate on four levels – levels of the snake, the jaguar, the hummingbird, and the eagle. The snake is about cold-blooded and rational survival and quest for security. My time with my Banker was the time of the snake. In a quest for security, I sought money, power, and career success. The jaguar is about the emotions, pleasure, and sensuality. My Chef provided me the full range of these.

The hummingbird, however, engages life at the soul level.

Did you know that this tiny bird migrates from Canada to Brazil every year? When you engage life at this level, a house is not just a house but a home. Your spouse is not just a roommate you share domestic responsibilities with, but a soulmate. At this level, you are able to see the deeper meaning behind the physical world and understand that life is an epic journey, just like the hummingbird's migration with its share of ups and downs. My time as a single mom in search of love and purpose was the time of the hummingbird.

Finally, eagles… Eagles can fly high above the mountains and see a small mouse scurrying on the valley floor. Eagles are healers, and provide a light for those around them, because they know that behind the highest mountain peaks lie the deepest valleys.

I have, in the end, found meaning in my heartache by gaining perspective and learning to release the rejection, resentment, and regret I have harbored in my heart. Now I am able to feel deep gratitude for my Banker, my Chef, and my Healer. Because it was the love of these men that helped me grow to be the woman I am today. As the renowned mystic and poet of love Rumi suggests, our lovers are truly a reflection of who we are inside.

The Seer

With the love and support of my Healer, my passions and purpose shifted as I evolved and shed beliefs that did not serve me. I was no longer fulfilled by a six-figure pay check, social status, and physical pleasure, but did not know where to go from there. So I decided to embark on a Vision Quest to discover my unique gift for the world.

For those who are unfamiliar, a Vision Quest is a ritual of the Native Indians and other ancient shamanic cultures, undertaken by those seeking divine messages by forgoing worldly comforts of shelter, food, and sometimes even water in solitude in the wild. Jesus Christ's wandering in the desert for 40 days and 40 nights was a kind of Vision Quest.

After so many workshops, trainings and healing sessions, I came to the conclusion that I could not find the answers I was seeking from an external source. I realized I needed to tap into the divine source of wisdom within me. In the arid Aravaipa Canyon of Arizona, I embarked on a journey of self-discovery. During my three nights in the wilderness beseeching the Creator for answers, I was given the name Shadow Cat Moon Dancer. In my weakened state, I wasn't quite sure what this actually meant. I just thought it was kind of a cool spiritual name. It took years for this name to unfold in my life. Shadow cats, often considered bad luck due to their association with spirits (or disembodied energy assemblages as I know them), were considered messengers from beyond, and were believed to walk between the worlds. Moon Dancing, I found out later, was also a shamanic ritual undertaken under either the new or full moon to travel between realms for guidance and wisdom.

Having been a banker and corporate executive, I did not immediately embrace my spiritual gifts, because I feared judgement from others. I didn't want to become one of the woo-woo types who lost their marbles! This led me to another journey of voraciously reading books on quantum physics, depth psychology, epigenetics, and neuroscience. My logical mind had to be persuaded of the validity of the metaphysical phenomenon I was experiencing and not dismiss or invalidate it as a figment of my imagination. Einstein said: "Imagination is more important than knowledge. For knowledge is limited, whereas imagination embraces the entire world, stimulating progress, giving birth to evolution. The true sign of intelligence is not knowledge but imagination." I had now come to a point that I was able to see the deep wisdom in these words.

Until now, the trainings and studies were for my own healing and growth. Having held traditional corporate jobs most of my career, I never really thought that being a healer or guide would be my path. Despite my ego's resistance, I slowly relented to my Soul's desires to be a guide for those going through the dark night of the soul. The moment I let go of judgement, my intuitive abilities came rapidly. My deepest joy came when I was helping others in their journey towards transformation. Helping my friends, and eventually my clients, break free of old patterns and emerge into their empowered true selves was deeply rewarding work.

The desire for love and affection is the most fundamental human need. Love makes the world go around and is critical for our emotional and physical well-being. I also believe it is absolutely the foundation for all other personal transformational work to bring one to wholeness. It's no wonder that when working with my clients, I have noticed that given an array of life challenges, the lack of love was undoubtedly the most distressing for the soul. My greatest wish and purpose for writing this book is to assist those who are seeking a fulfilling romantic relationship prepare themselves to experience true love.

The MAGNETIC Process

In the following chapters, I have outlined eight basic principles based on modern science and ancient esoteric wisdom on how to attract the right partner and nurture that attraction into a meaningful and fulfilling relationship. The eight principles are divided into three parts – 1) Relating Inwards, 2) Relating to the Beloved, and 3) Relating to Your Space. Here's a preview of what you'll find in the rest of the book:

Part 1: Relating Inwards

The process starts with how to relate to ourselves.

Principle 1: Mind Your Elements

Our natural constitution is a very good indicator of our emotional, mental, and physical tendencies. Ancient healers across the world have used the natural elements as blueprints to understand the human constitution and disposition. As such, we will start with the exploration of the self by first understanding how the natural elements influence our love lives.

Principle 2: Acknowledge and Release Ghosts of the Past

Our lovers are reflections of who we are, and as such, we must clean house for the best possible outcome. We will explore how to clear the ghosts of the past by releasing rejection, resentment, and regret.

Principle 3: Greet and Transform the Demons Within

We will then delve deeper into the path of self-awareness by identifying the inner demons that lurk in our shadows. Specifically, these are our belief patterns that prevent us from freely receiving and giving love.

Principle 4: Navigate and Nourish Your Body

We will examine how we relate to our bodies and the beliefs that we hold about our bodies. We will learn how to work with the body to get clear on what we want, as well as how to tap into our femininity and sensuality.

Part 2: Relating to the Beloved

Now that we have gone through a course of purging, we will take a look at what men want and how romantic attraction works.

Principle 5: Edify and Elucidate

Here, we will begin to understand how men are different from women and appreciate them for who they are. We will explore how best to express our thoughts and emotions with our man. We will examine the differences in how women and men communicate and strategies to best bridge these potential gaps through lessons in clear and compassionate communication.

Principle 6: Tempt and Tease

We will look at how attraction works on a biological, emotional, and metaphysical level. According to scientists, what we think of as conscious decisions are not very conscious at all. Examining levels of brainwave activity, neuroscientists have learned that our conscious decisions are made 2-3 seconds prior to when we consciously think we have. (Nørretranders, *The User Illusion*) What does this mean for choosing our mates? What drives us to be attracted to one person over another? We have all experienced the pull towards the wrong guy at least once, and despite our inner alarm bells, we can be drawn like moths to a flame. Why are we drawn to some while repelled by others? To give us the best odds for lasting love, we will explore the forces of attraction.

Part 3: Relating to Your Space

Principle 7: Illuminate Your Guilt

As women, we go through three distinct phases of life – maid, mother, and crone. Our bodies, emotions, and social responsibilities evolve during these various stages. At each stage, whatever the circumstance, so many women profess to be guilty – either of not being there for their children because of their careers or other obligations. This chapter illuminates the true identity of this guilt that cages us and our loved ones.

Principle 8: Create a Supportive Environment

Your environment – which is your family, community, and the spaces you live and work in – has an impact on your psyche. Here, I introduce several tools to help create an environment that supports your desire for healing and lasting love.

I recommend that you read the whole book in order and do the recommended exercises instead of skipping ahead. I also suggest that you keep a journal while reading to track and reflect on your progress. In your daily writings, make note of the following:

- Pay attention to your dreams,
- Track your thoughts, especially those that recur frequently,
- Notice your emotions and how they impact your body.

Now, let's get started!

PART I

Relating Inwards

CHAPTER 3
Mind Your Element

*"Look deep into nature and then you will understand
everything better."*
-EINSTEIN

All ancient healing traditions from India, Tibet, China, Native Indian tribes to the Greeks believed that our bodies are made up of a combination of natural elements. Using nature as a model, these traditions were able to understand the human mental, emotional, and physical constitution and successfully develop tools to balance the elements and thus heal the body and mind. Ayurvedic and Chinese medicine are two lineages that withstood the test of time and are still practiced actively into modern times. Here, I have combined several of these systems to create a new universal system of seven elements.

Understanding your personal make-up of these elements will give you insight into your own personal love language, beliefs, possible pitfalls, and an understanding of how to avoid them. You can find the interactive assessment at my website www.sukisohn.com/quiz to find out your make-up. Here is an overview of the seven elements:

Fire – Passionate and Impulsive

A woman with the predominant fire element tends to be of lean and wiry build. She is extroverted with a generally positive outlook on life. She is passionate, feisty, emotionally volatile, and has strong likes and dislikes. Though she is quick to anger, she does not hold grudges. Sex is very important to her. She likely follows her gut instincts, and her heart and head play second fiddle. She attracts men easily but may have a harder time getting them to stick around or stay committed. Her motto is, "If you got it, flaunt it." She likes to be noticed and will go to lengths to make sure that her presence is appreciated. She seems outwardly confident but has a deep need to be validated by others. She also tends to be impulsive and reactive. Love for a fire woman is all-consuming and filled with physical pleasure and desire. Her love block is her impulsive nature and mistaking lust for love.

Air – Joyful and Flighty

A woman ruled by the air element is pixie-like, cheerful, and flighty. She is generally of slim and delicate build and does not put on weight easily. She is extroverted and friendly but fickle. Like the wind, her feelings change quickly and she tends to get bored easily. She can be on edge and nervous when stressed, is often fidgety, and has an eternally childlike quality. Her motto would be, "Girls just want to have fun." Her flighty nature makes her likely to either run away or "play dumb" and pretend not to see obvious problems in a relationship. Love for air women is sweet, tender, and joyful. Her love block is her belief that commitment will compromise her freedom.

Earth – Dependable and Stubborn

An earth element woman is nurturing and caring. She is introverted, calm, grounded, and maternal. She is likely to have a medium to a more voluptuous build. She is also practical and steady in her approach to life and love. She is reliable and compassionate. She tends to get complacent, lazy, and may become very stubborn. "Slow and steady wins the race," would be her motto. She has a tendency to bend over backwards to accommodate her lover, friends, and family at the expense of herself. She can become obsessive and intrusive and can worry unnecessarily. Also, her wish to be needed sometimes leads her into co-dependent relationships or makes her give too much and become depleted. Love for an earth woman is bonding in mind, body, and soul. Her love block is that she can become smothering and even controlling in the name of love.

Water – Intuitive and Emotional

The water element woman is reserved and cool on the surface, but her emotions run deep. This gives her a mysterious and enigmatic air about her. She is highly self-sufficient and independent. She can go with the flow and be supple, but also has a strong will to get things done. Unlike the wood types, who get things done by force, the water type is more adaptable and subtle, and can achieve her goals by ascertaining the best path to her desired outcome. She is introverted and appreciates solitude and tranquillity. She is likely of medium or round build. She is seductive and highly intuitive and empathic. She is most likely to follow her heart, but may completely ignore her head and gut when she falls in love. She does not forgive or forget easily, and at worst can be vindictive and jealous. She can isolate herself and become cold and unresponsive when hurt. Love for a water woman is the joining of two streams, where you become your lover and your lover becomes you. Her love block is that she gets too swept up in her emotions and loses perspective.

Metal – Disciplined and Judgmental

A metal element woman is detail-oriented, methodical, and a perfectionist. She is faithful, brave, and magnanimous. She is also intellectually sharp and has a high level of self-discipline, making her highly successful in her career. She likes structure and organization. She likes to "cut to the chase" and is direct in her communication but can also be very charming and diplomatic. Metal types often have a strong athletic build. Though she is no wallflower, she is generally introverted and can seem insular. She tends to hold on to grief and past hurts that can damage her present relationships. This can make her guarded and unwilling to open up and end up replacing intimacy with material possessions, or focus solely on career success. Love for a metal woman is completion. Her love block is her critical and judgmental nature.

Wood – Expansive and Impatient

A wood element woman is competitive and thrives when challenged. She can be both extroverted and introverted. She is also compassionate and philanthropic. Wood types are determined, type-A personalities who do well under pressure and seek adventure, novelty, and movement. She is constantly looking to grow and evolve. Wood types tend to have thin, lean bodies and move with grace. She needs to feel a sense of purpose in her life. She works hard to achieve her goals but can drive herself to exhaustion. Wood types can be irritable, frustrated, and impatient. She can be overly stubborn and set in her ways. Love for a wood type woman is expansion and evolution. Her love block is that she can be pushy and likes to bend others to her will.

Spirit - Compassionate and Universal

Spirit is the pure life force that is the source of all of the above elements. Similar to how white light can be fractioned to produce the colors of the rainbow, the other six elements have arisen from the original pure life force of Spirit. The Taoists call this Chi; the Vedic traditions of India call it Prana. While the other elements are of the physical realm, Spirit is metaphysical. When combined with other elements it allows an eagle-eye perspective that brings out the best of the element it is fused with. It manifests as awareness, and when fully integrated, allows one to understand the nature of the mind and human experience. Her love block is that being self-sufficient and whole on her own, she unconsciously may not find romantic love necessary.

Many of us are a combination of these elements. If that's the case for you, read the two or three elements you scored highest on to understand your relationship pitfalls and what makes you attractive. In Chapter 5, we will further explore common beliefs held by each elemental type that may be holding back your ability to have a fulfilling intimate relationship.

Following are some examples of how the elements combine to create personalities, each with their own unique allure and love blocks.

Jenna's main elements were metal, wood, and fire. She was a perfectionist, driven to succeed, and was a bold and vocal force to be reckoned with. Her strong metal element made her hold herself and others to a high standard, which often made her highly critical and cutting. The wood element instilled an adventurous spirit and tireless ambition to grow. Metal, wood and fire are all masculine elements. This combination often results in a woman who is highly accomplished and successful in the workplace but her lack of feminine qualities make it challenging to find and keep a romantic partner. Women like Jenna often attract a man who is more feminine and yielding. She is typically the one who wears the pants in the relationship and she likes it that way, yet at the same time, she can be critical and disrespectful of her partner for being too sensitive or a pushover.

Maria was predominantly of the fire element but with a touch of air and earth. The fire element made her a passionate sexy bombshell and the air element added to the fickle and impulsive nature of fire. At the same time, the earth element made her a very caring and giving individual. The paradoxical combination of the self-centered fire and self-effacing earth meant that she attracted men with her sexy appearance and but ended up giving away too much too soon.

Nora scored highly with spirit followed by air and water. She was calm and highly intuitive but lacked motivation and unconsciously didn't want to be of this world. Spirit, air and water are the more mutable and metaphysical elements. Lacking balance of the more physical elements of metal, earth, and wood, she was hermit-like and withdrawn into her own stories and beliefs. Also, the emotional nature of the water made her more likely to hold on to past regrets and resentments.

As you can see, understanding your elemental nature provides good insight into your own mental and emotional make up. You can find a quick assessment of your elements at www.sukisohn.com/quiz. If you would like to go into a more in-depth analysis apply for a complimentary Seven Element Discovery Session at www.sukisohn.com/apply.

CHAPTER 4

Acknowledge and Release Ghosts of the Past

"The wound is where the Light enters you."
-RUMI

This book does not offer short-term Band-Aid solutions. The primary purpose of this book is to help you find true love. As such, we need to start by taking out your garbage.

I once dated a man named Diego who I met during a ski trip to Aspen. I met him at a party and never thought the relationship would amount to much – and sure enough, it didn't, despite the fact that this man's intentions toward me were honest and true. I was shut down and unable to make myself available to him. I was haunted by my past hurts and was too busy protecting myself to be present, let alone fall in love. He said to me, "I would move mountains to win your heart, but I cannot fight ghosts." I was not seeing Diego for who he was or what he was offering me. Instead, I was protecting myself by projecting onto him all the negative traits of my past lovers. I was constantly waiting for him to do something wrong, and of course I found plenty of things that were wrong with him – but not because of any fault of his. I then realized that I will always find what I seek. The relationship did not last long, but his words were an epiphany for me.

No man can fight the ghosts of your past and win. Releasing these ghosts is *your* job. So what exactly are these ghosts? The primary feelings you feel towards past failed relationships are rejection, resentment, and regret. Holding on to rejection, protecting yourself at all costs, stems from a sense of fear and possibly shame of not being worthy of love, which in turn prevents you from being able to open up to intimacy and love. Resentment is an expression of anger. This anger may be toward your past lovers, but most likely it is toward yourself. Finally, there's regret, which is born of grief and sadness. Regret is born from a critical voice that lacks self-compassion and keeps us in a state of guilt, feeling unworthy. In some cases, women even believe they need to be punished with a loveless life for their mistakes.

How do you release these ghosts? It starts by recognizing them for what they are. They are ghosts created in your mind. They are not of the present moment, but energetic imprints of the past in our mind and body. Once you recognize that these feelings and thoughts were created in your own mind, you can shift your perspective of the story from the position of victim to one of creator. It is very common to feel resistance to the idea that you were the one who created the hurts of the past. However, radical acceptance and taking ownership of all experiences is the key to unlocking your power to transform your life.

Once you accept that you created these ghosts, you can transform them. How? By recognizing the lesson behind these past hurts. What would be the silver lining behind every hurt? What did it enable you to do? What positive traits did it develop in you that you did not have before? If you are holding on to any of the big three Rs (rejection, resentment, and regret) and you're continuing to re-enact similar patterns in your present relationships, you probably have not learned the lesson that the universe and your soul sought to teach you.

How We Create Our Own Reality

Discoveries in quantum physics have revealed how our reality is created through our consciousness. In the famous Double Slit Experiment, physicists discovered that light can display characteristics of waves or particles, and that the determining factor was the *observer*. In this experiment, a light was shined at a panel with two slits and another panel behind it to capture the pattern created by the light shining through the slits. Scientists expected the pattern to be two lines mimicking the two slits on the first panel. But to their surprise, the second panel showed two cloudy shapes, suggesting that instead of traveling in a straight line as you would expect a particle would do, the light behaved like a wave, capturing all potential movements. They did the experiment again, this time *observing* the movement of the light from beginning to end. This time, the light did indeed display two lines like they had originally anticipated.

I apologize if this is too heady and geeky for some. So let me get to the crux of it. Through this experiment, scientists concluded that the *observer's* intentions and expectations manifested the pattern they expected to see the light produce. In other words, the *observer's* beliefs collapsed all of the infinite potential of outcomes into the one that they expected to see. As Einstein had said, "Reality is merely an illusion, though a very persistent one."

One summer I had planned a long vacation in Hawaii with my mother. We have always had a difficult relationship, and we could not go three days without fighting. I was apprehensive about my time with her. But a week prior to leaving for my planned vacation, I heard a lecture from a Kabbalist about how it is our own beliefs that keep us from being able manifest a more positive outcome for ourselves. I decided to experiment with this and consciously dropped all preconceptions I had about my mother.

I visualized shattering the past perspective I had of my mother, and to my surprise, we had a wonderful time together. Einstein also famously said, "Insanity is doing the same thing over and over again and expecting a different result." Shift yourself and see what unfolds. Your past is not your future.

Resentment

My husband of seven years had cheated on me. We went through couples' therapy, but that didn't really work out because, unbeknownst to me, he never stopped seeing the other woman. Naturally this led to bitter divorce proceedings that lasted years. After many thousands of dollars of legal fees and drawn-out arguments, I felt deep resentment towards my ex. I did my best to be civil towards him in front of my son, but the anger I felt was always just below the surface, about to burst. What I didn't realize was that this resentment was keeping me safe from feeling *hurt* by my ex. I was using the energy created by the anger and resentment as a shield to protect myself from emotions I did not want to face, such as rejection and regret. I was too proud to admit that I was hurting.

If you are harboring resentment towards your ex or any other person in your life, can you see how that resentment is protecting you? Can you see what the side effects of this protective shield are? The counter-intuitive antidote to resentment is being open to vulnerability.

My relationship with Diego was a good example of how my resentment towards past lovers made me highly defensive and critical of any love interest. The burden was on him to *prove* to me that he was different while I was constantly picking apart his behavior trying to find why he was all wrong. It takes two to tango. Both partners need to be open, engaged and committed to make a relationship work.

Rejection

Fear of rejection can no doubt prevent us from having the love we want. In fact, it creates a picture of failure in your mind even before you can make that first tentative step toward love.

Fear of rejection is generally a pattern that originates before your adult romantic relationships. I find that it often started in childhood, mostly in relation to our parents. Go back to the time you first felt a sense of rejection. What beliefs did you absorb from that experience? Can you see what lessons were being taught to you through that rejection? My first sense of rejection was with my mother. My mother was a critical woman, and her way of expressing love was to constantly push me towards some unachievable goal of perfection. I carried the belief that I had to be "perfect" to be lovable into my romantic relationships. This created a rigidity and a sharpness in my heart. Fortunately, I came to realize the lesson in my experience of rejection from my mother was to appreciate and accept myself just the way I am. In the end, I realized that I did not need to be validated by my mother – or any another person for that matter.

Self-worth can only come from within. Self-worth derived from external validation will always be temporary and constantly fleeting. The key to releasing fear of rejection is true self-acceptance, warts and all!

Regret

A common obstacle to self-acceptance is regret. We all regret something we have done in the past. It is an inevitable fact of life that at one point or another we have been disappointed with ourselves. We become our own worst critics, which further drives us away from self-acceptance and appreciation. In my moments of clarity, which came years after burning through anger and resentment, I was able to see how I had contributed to the demise of my marriage. Could I forgive myself for having been so wrapped up in my own needs that I failed to see how this was hurting my husband and our marriage? It takes a certain level of maturity to process through the immediate and urgent feelings of anger and fear before we can focus on the sense of regret and forgiveness. Regret can be a doorway to a deeper perspective, but if you linger in that doorway too long, you can get caught up in the trap of regret that may lead you to believe your past actions make you unworthy of love.

Which of the three Rs (resentment, rejection, or regret) are you most haunted by? Your love personality type (fire, water, air, earth, metal, wood and spirit) will most likely dictate your natural inclinations. Once you have identified which of the three you feel compelled to work on, you can learn to release it via the following exercise. You may find that you want to do the exercise for all three, and that's perfectly fine. Now let's get down to business and start taking out your garbage.

EXERCISE: Hoi'Oponopono

The indigenous Hawaiians used this following exercise to resolve conflicts peacefully in their tribes. Traditionally, it was a twelve-step ceremony conducted by the tribal chief for two arguing parties. However, it is also an excellent tool to release negative emotions and judgement to achieve inner peace.

1. Think of the situation or person that gets you riled up, causes you sorrow, or any other strong emotion that is eating you up.
2. Now say the following words:

> *I am sorry.*
> *Please forgive me.*
> *Thank you.*
> *I love you.*

3. Keep repeating the words until you feel a sense of peace and love in your heart and feel your body relax.

You may find that saying these words is very difficult for you, especially if you have been at the receiving end of abuse, infidelity, abandonment, or rejection. When you are saying "I am sorry. Please forgive me," you are saying this from your higher self. This is the part of you that's no longer limited by your own story, but able to see how you have contributed to unpleasantness, bad blood, and anger to humanity as a whole. It is an exercise to release any feelings of judgement, blame, or fault. In the end, these feelings hurt you much more than anyone else.

Accessing the Power of Now

Rejection, resentment, and regret are projections of the mind that keep us trapped in the past instead of the learning from these experiences to improve our present moment and future.

The mind, unlike the body, is free of time and space. The disparity between the body and the mind can create negative emotions and behaviors. If your mind is in the future while your body is in the present moment, you'll feel anxiety and sometimes fear about the future. When your mind is stuck in the past, you often feel regret and guilt. In contrast, if your mind is in the present *with* the body, you are able to gaze to the future with hope. Similarly, with the mind and body anchored to the present, you can reach back and access wisdom from your past experiences. The body can only be in the present, and thus is the tool for you to access the power of the present moment.

You can't do anything about the past or some imaginary future you fear. The only time you can take action and influence our life is in the now. Increasing body awareness is one way to bring your mind to the present moment. From the present moment, you are able to manage the melodrama created by the mind in reaction to rejection, resentment, and regret. When you find yourself stuck in negative emotions, check where your mind has wandered off to and gently bring it back it to the present moment with your breath.

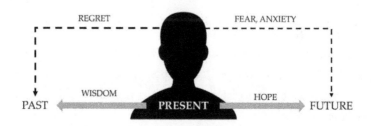

Figure 1: Body-Mind Disparity

EXERCISE: Brain Wave Vibration

Our autonomic nervous system (ANS) is responsible for all basic metabolic functions for sustaining life, most of which we are unconscious of. The autonomic nervous system has two branches: the sympathetic nervous system and the parasympathetic nervous system. The sympathetic nervous system is the "fight or flight" system, while the parasympathetic nervous system is the "rest and digest" system. From a physiological point of view, these systems work in opposition. When the sympathetic system is activated, that is when we are threatened, our pupils dilate, blood is pumped away from major organs to large muscles to fight or flee. On the other hand, when the threat is removed and we are able to let our guard down, the parasympathetic system kicks in to relax, recover, and rejuvenate. The blood is pumped back towards to the major organs and the pupils contract. While the beta brainwave (focused) is associated with sympathetic system, the alpha, theta, and delta are associated with the parasympathetic state. Reiki and other quantum healers are known to be in alpha and theta waves when they conduct healings.

This is a Korean Taoist exercise that allows us to get us into alpha and theta brainwave state by bringing our minds back to the present moment. Make sure you pay attention to the sensations in your body as you do this exercise.

1. Take a comfortable seat with your back straight and close your eyes.
2. Make a gentle fist with your thumb curled in under your other fingers. (This act alone starts calming the brain, as the pad of thumb corresponds to the pituitary gland, the master gland that regulates all other glands.)
3. With the pinky side of your fist start tapping two inches below your belly button.
4. Focus your attention so you can feel the vibration created by the tapping in your womb.
5. As you continue the tapping, slowly start swaying your head side to side like you're saying no. This will gently release your spine.
6. Continue doing this for 10-20 minutes.

I have created a Spotify playlist to aid this exercise consisting primarily of traditional Asian drum music. Repetitive drum beats have been used in many ancient cultures to induce a hypnotic trance state of theta brainwaves. You can find the link on my website: www.sukisohn.com/resources

Seeing Life Challenges as a Gift

Gaining a broader perspective beyond our own stories is the key to releasing the ghost of rejection, resentment, and regret.

There are two basic attitudes towards all difficult life experiences. First is that our life events happen by random chance, and we as feeble humans do our best to face the challenges that come our way. The second, which is my personal view towards life, is that all experiences have a purpose – especially the hard ones.

One of my favorite movies of all times is *The Matrix*. In the movie, humans are raised in pods that are plugged into the Matrix, a program that simulates normal human life. There is scene where Mr. Anderson, the evil nemesis A.I., explains to Neo, our human hero and savior, that at first the Matrix was created as a utopia with no pain or challenges, but this led to massive failure of this crop of humans. Apparently, humans needed hardship to grow and thrive.

The same is true for trees. Trees that have survived through drought, floods, and harsh weather grow resilient by anchoring deeper into the earth. Trees that have not faced such hardship on a regular basis do not last long, as the first harsh storm can uproot them. You may choose to believe that you are the victim of happenstance, or you may to choose to believe that you are the creator of your own life who invites and accepts all experiences – including the heartache. Choose to accept life as it is, with all its ups and downs, as a gift that allows you to evolve into a better person. Because what is the alternative? Living life as a victim, powerless to affect any change to your circumstances. After all, the lotus flower blooms most beautifully from the deepest and thickest mud.

EXERCISE: Managing the Emotional Flood

Here you might be saying, "Easier said than done." What about the emotions that flood us and pull us back to negative thought patterns, seemingly before we can make a conscious decision? Einstein said, "We can't solve problems by using the same kind of thinking we used when we created them." Essentially, we need to be able to create some distance from the emotion we are experiencing.

Ancient traditions have always understood the power of words. Words have powerful impact on our brains, and our language shows insights into how our whole culture thinks and relates towards its emotions. In English, we use the verb "to be" to express an emotion – I am sad, I am angry, I am happy, etc. – we also use the verb "to be" to identify who we are – I am Susan, I am Nancy, etc. In other words, we identify with our emotions in the English language.

However, we are not our emotions. Following is a simple exercise that allows us to cultivate neutrality to emotions through the power of words.

1. Close your eyes and take a few deep breaths.
2. Think of an incident that made you very angry.
3. Bring yourself to the moment and let the emotion flood your body, so you can feel the heat rise and your body tense up.
4. Repeat the words, "I am angry."
5. Notice how this effects your body. Notice where you feel tightness, heat, and discomfort.
6. Now repeat the words: "I have feelings of anger."
7. Keep on repeating these words until you feel a shift in the sensations of your body.
8. Try to notice the changes you feel in your body and mind simply by changing your words.

CHAPTER 5

Greet and Transform Your Demons

*"It is better to conquer yourself than to win a thousand battles.
Then the victory is yours. It cannot be taken from you, not by
angels or by demons, heaven or hell."*

-BUDDHA

Now that we have taken care of ghosts of the past, it is time to focus on the negative belief and behavioral patterns that are imprinted in our brain in the present. Our lives are shaped by the decisions we make. But who or what is really making those decisions? Neuroscientists found that brain activity spikes seconds before any conscious decision or action is taken. Furthermore, what comes into our conscious awareness is a tiny sliver of all the information the brain receives. While our brain receives 11 million bits per second from the world to our sensory mechanisms, our conscious mind only processes about 18 bits of data per second (Nørretranders, *The User Illusion*).

The mechanism that filters this data is "programming" in the forms of social conditioning, DNA, and soul memories. Naturally, there is subconscious programming that affects your ability to give and receive love. Free will seems to be a myth at this point. But there is hope. Our unique human ability to meta-cognate – to be aware of our own thought process – allows us to change our programming. There are countless "programs" that affect our ability to connect to one another. These programs are like spells that keep us trapped in their confines. Here, I will discuss six of them.

Defense Mechanisms

Let's start with defense mechanisms.

The brain is wired to avoid pain, and as such, your defense mechanisms are some of the most insidious programs that can negatively impact your relationships. These are programs that protect us from getting hurt. There are three types of defense mechanisms that women use in relating to men.

First is the *Man Hater*. These women use hostility towards men to protect themselves. They use blanket statements like, "All men cheat," "Chivalry is dead," "Men are pigs," "There are no good men out there." They are often emotionally shut down and distrustful of men. Their cynicism towards men and romance in general pushes away would-be suitors both literally and energetically. Failing to recognize their own part in their circumstances, they continue to blame men for the woes of their life. Generally, women who have just gone through a bitter divorce or breakup find themselves here at one point or another. Out of balance water and metal element women are most likely to fall into this trap.

Second is the *Man Eater*. Her defense mechanism leads her to falsely believe that women are superior to men. She tends to be promiscuous, taking lovers as it pleases her. "Boy Toy" would be one of her coined phrases. Think of Samantha in *Sex and City*. Her outwardly confident and domineering attitude is her way of protecting herself. In some cases, she confuses lust and passion for intimacy. She tends to jump right into bed without allowing a deeper relationship to develop. As times passes and her desire for some level of commitment emerges, she will either run from these feelings and end the relationship or wonder why her lover does not want to commit, when it was *her* who set up the stage that way.

My client Maria was a Man Eater, unbeknownst to herself. She constantly found herself in many hot, steamy romantic dalliances that didn't go anywhere. She didn't understand why she continued to attract unavailable men until she became aware of her subconscious belief: "Men are toys." Once she was able to release this belief, within months she met a man who became her husband. Out of balance fire and wood women are most likely to fall into this category.

The third type is the *Man Server*. These women bend over backwards to please their partners. Think of a teenage girl who relents to having sex just to keep the boy she is interested in. She uses being nice and accommodating as a defense mechanism to avoid confrontation and potential rejection. Guilt and subtle manipulation is her weapon of choice. She has beliefs like, "I have to be a good girl to be lovable." She may even feel that women are inferior to men. Women who come from patriarchal cultures often carry this belief. Out of balance earth and air element women are most likely to be in this category.

Addiction to Drama

We, as a society, are addicted to drama to some level or another.

The brain constantly seeks to expand and experience new things. Modern society offers constant and sensational stimulation in forms of numerous entertainment options, multiple mobile devices, various social media channels, and an abundance of information in general. We live in a society that is constantly "on". We see in children the rise of ADD and other behavioural problems. Adults have not been able to escape the impact of the fast-moving information age especially in our relationships. America's obsession with celebrities and drama-filled reality TV shows is an indication of our society's need to escape the tedium of the mundane to make life "interesting".

Despite claims of wanting a nurturing and supportive relationship, many women are addicted to the emotional intensity of drama. The rush they experience from the self-created drama is like a drug to them. The thought of a calm, caring relationship feels positively boring and flat. Like an adrenaline junkie in search of the next high, women who are addicted to drama create situations that result in emotional intensity. In a way, this makes them feel alive. They are often easily distracted and may even have some level of ADD.

Karla is a good example of this addiction to drama. She was recently divorced with three kids. She was a successful fashion designer and was hooked on the emotional intensity of the industry and colorful characters who were her colleagues. She couldn't stand to be bored at work, and certainly not by a man. This led her to attract men who met her subconscious desire for drama. Her ex-husband whom she had three children with turned out to be gay!

What is underlying this addiction is these women's inability to be present. When you are unable to be present with yourself, it is very difficult to truly connect to another. For clients like this, I would highly recommend a meditation routine to increase the brain's ability to focus and tame the monkey mind. Due to their naturally outward and expansive nature; fire, air, and wood elementals are most susceptible to addiction to drama.

I Am Not Enough

Another prevalent belief is simply, "I am not enough."

Having been raised by a metal element mother with her critical perfectionist standards, I always felt that I was not enough. I felt that if I let go for a moment, all would go to hell in a handbasket, so I had to be constantly vigilant. I also held the belief that it was this drive towards perfection made me a better person, thus was deeply invested in holding on to my belief that I was never enough.

During my time as a struggling single mom, my mother, quite out of the blue, said to me; you know you are more attractive, smarter, and capable than most. You don't have to try so hard. These words hit me like lightening. Quite frankly, I didn't even realize that I was working so hard to be lovable.

We seem to have so many reasons why we are not enough for love. I am not skinny enough. I am not feminine enough. I am not pretty enough. I am not young enough. I am not smart enough. And the list goes on. The truth is that we are all enough for love.

Love is that force within us that accepts a person with all their shortcomings. You do not attract love by being or finding the perfect person. Rather, real love emerges from your ability to see perfection in the *imperfections* in yourself and others. So how could imperfections, whatever they may be, ever prevent you from love? Your flaws are perfect for the heart that is meant to love you. If you still believe that you are not enough for love, you are confusing infatuation, lust, or perhaps envy for love.

Hidden Narcissism

Another blind spot for many is hidden narcissism, a tendency to be self-obsessed ironically at the expense of our self-confidence.

Susan was beautiful, tall, blonde, and slim. She was a model in her twenties and her looks have always been important to her. As she grew older, she started to feel more insecure about her looks. This greatly affected her confidence. For Susan it was her looks, but for others it may be intelligence, style, or career success that they obsess over.

Many people experience dating jitters. The kind of thoughts that run through their minds during these times are, "Does my hair look okay?"; "Do I look fat in this dress?"; "Do I sound smart?"; "Does he find me attractive?" With this kind of frame of mind, you are utterly trapped in the Me-world. You are unable to direct your attention to the person in front of you. It then becomes impossible to create a real connection with another human being. What could be more boring and unattractive than a self-absorbed narcissist? Next time you feel the dating jitters, shift your attention to your date and become genuinely interested in the person in front of you instead of obsessing over your hair or outfit.

Genetic Lineage Promises

Some women seem to unconsciously carry out a family legacy.

Rima's grandmother was physically abused by her husband. Her mother was raped by her father after they separated. Rima has now gone through two marriages with verbally abusive men.

Epigenetics is the study of how the environment and individual lifestyle can also directly interact with the genome to influence gene expression. In other words, current life experiences can alter DNA with multi-generational consequences (Lipton, *Biology of Belief*). Awareness of this subconscious programming derived from genetic legacy is the first step towards transforming it.

Renowned cellular biologist and author Bruce Lipton says, "Just like a single cell, the character of our lives is determined not by our genes but by our responses to the environmental signals that propel life." If you happen to be unconsciously living out a tragic family legacy, like my client Rima, you know that it does not have to be that way. Once Rima recognized the genetic patterns exhibited by her mother and grandmother she was living out, and that she could be the one to break this chain for her unborn children and generations to come, she was very determined to make drastic changes in her life.

Your ability to proactively change your reaction to any circumstance is the kind of stuff that can alter your own DNA – not only for yourself but your offspring. Even the ones that have already been born, since children naturally model their parents unconsciously, and the environment you provide for them is certainly influencing their genes.

Karmic Past

Much like DNA, there can be soul memories that shape our beliefs and behavior. Irrational fears or aversions may be an indication of soul memories coming through.

Sometimes we meet people with whom we have an instant connection. You feel like you have known the person from a past life. It is very possible that this is the case. However, this does not necessarily mean that this person is your soulmate. I see women get confused and rattled by meeting someone like this even though the person is obviously unavailable. We do carry soul memories into this life. However, often the sense of connection comes from a place of familiarity, a comfort zone for the soul, not true love.

I once worked with a woman who had an irrational dislike of Spain and even the Spanish language. During one of our sessions, we discovered one of her past lives as a Jewish woman persecuted during the Spanish Inquisition. I met another woman who disliked tall blonde men. It turned out that she was a victim of Viking raid in her past life.

Katherine was a professor in psychology who was intrigued by the idea of past lives. I met her at a conference where Brian Weiss, former head of the Psychology Department at Mt. Sinai and author of *Many Lives, Many Masters*, was giving a talk on his experiences and offering a group past life regression session. She was sitting next to me during the conference and had an unapproachable air about her. It was obvious that, though she was curious, she was highly skeptical. Then, during the past life regression meditation, she started crying uncontrollably. I was surprised to see this cold, buttoned-up woman break down like that. After the session, I leaned over and asked if she was okay. She said yes, and asked if I would have lunch with her. During lunch, she told me that she didn't believe in any of this "stuff" and never had an experience like this. She then went on to tell me about the past life she saw during the session.

It was just at the beginning WWI. She saw herself as a young woman at the train station sending her fiancé off to war. He never came back, and she was heart-broken. She never married and vowed to never love again. Soul promises like that can carry over to multiple lives. In this lifetime, she was a highly educated and attractive woman. She was in her mid-fifties and had never married, but was never short of suitors. She came from a loving family and her parents were happily married. She didn't have any traumatic experiences with men, so she always wondered if there was something wrong with her. She consciously desired to meet a nice man, get married, and have kids – but it never happened for her. After this vision, everything made sense to her. She realized she was never able to open her heart in an intimate relationship because of this soul promise made in a past life.

Michelle was a single mom who got divorced from her physically and verbally abusive husband. She came from a happy family and was the apple of her father's eye. She was an accomplished doctor. During a guided meditation session with her, she spontaneously encountered a past life of hers as a Japanese "comfort woman" during WWII. She was 15 years old in this past life, and was considered one of the prettiest and smartest girls in her small town. She was proud and thought herself a notch above most. When the Japanese army came to "recruit" young girls to supposedly to work at factories in the city, she was excited and jumped at the opportunity. To her horror, this was a guise to find girls to work at army-operated brothels. She was raped, abused, and died bitter and broken. She recalls thinking that if she were a man this would have never happened. She was powerless because she was a woman.

Imprints from past lives can interfere with current lives. Our amnesia of these past lives lift for a reason. It is meant to give us a second chance to learn or remember a lesson from a former life. Sometimes remembering is enough to have a cathartic breakthrough like Katherine did. Michelle continued to work on her subconscious belief that she was powerless because she was a woman. She held deep distrust and resentment towards men, and her current life served to prove once again that men were not trustworthy. I worked with Michelle to release her soul's bitter karmic memories by helping her recognize that even in the direst of circumstances, the only person who can make her a victim is herself.

We cannot control our external circumstances, but how we react and perceive the experience is completely up to us. Many comfort women who survived the War became activists for women's rights causes. Though they were deceived and abused inhumanely, they did not die as victims. Michelle eventually remarried a wonderfully loving man and became an active supporter of non-profits working to end sex trafficking.

Side Note on Soulmates

Our souls seek to constantly evolve. Soulmates exist to help us along that process. Because these relationships are intended to help us grow, they are often challenging. Many people have unrealistic romantic notions about the idea of a soulmate relationship. Without reaching a certain level of maturity that enables us to see conflict and relationship challenges as growth opportunities, soulmate relationship will likely not last. Do they exist? Absolutely, but soulmate relationships are not for the faint of heart.

Tools to Identify Subconscious Beliefs

There are many false beliefs that we picked up as children, through society, through genes, and in some cases, through past lives. Many of these beliefs are completely unknown to us as they are deeply buried in our subconscious mind. Working with a trained healer who can elicit your own unique beliefs is powerful and transformative.

Before we move on to introducing the list of possible false beliefs, I would like to introduce a tool to access the unconscious mind through the body. Often, people are unconscious of the beliefs that they hold. In the 1970s, Dr. John Diamond discovered that muscles strengthen or weaken in the presence of positive or negative emotional and intellectual stimuli

(Hawkins, Power vs. Force). Positive statements and emotions made people strong, while negative ones made them weak. Your muscles are a built-in lie detector! Dr. David R. Hawkins took this to the next level in his book *Power vs. Force*. Dr. Hawkins refined the process and was able to create a progressive map of the human psyche: At the lowest level are shame and guilt, to joy, love, and enlightenment at the top.

Your body does not lie, and we can use this to uncover our hidden beliefs that are holding us back. There are several ways to test this muscle reaction, as discovered by Dr. John Diamond. Here are a couple of different methods:

If you have someone to help you with the test you can try one of these:

Partner Arm Press Method

1. Standing up, raise your non-dominant arm to the front parallel to the floor.
2. The tester then places one hand on the subject's other shoulder and two fingers of the other hand just above the subject's wrist of the extended arm.
3. Tester tells the subject to resist when tester tries to push the subject's arm down. Do this a few times for the test to calibrate strength of the subject.
4. Ask the subject to say "yes" and press the arm down. Next ask the subject to say "no" and press the arm down. The tester should pay special attention to the muscle's reaction with each answer. Once the muscle

response to "yes" and "no" is calibrated, you can start testing the beliefs listed below.

5. Ask the subject to say one of the beliefs. The tester then quickly presses down on the arm. If she stays strong, it means she believes the statement to be true. If she goes weak, she does not believe in the statement.

Press down at wrist with two fingers

Place other hand on shoulder

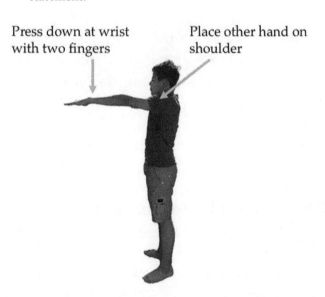

Partner Finger Method

Instead of using the arm, you can also use the fingers to test beliefs.

1. Have the subject make an "O" shape with thumb and index finger or the ring finger if the subject is very strong. The ring is the weakest finger, so testing can be done easier this way. Ask the subject to keep their fingers from being pulled apart.

2. Just like the arm raise method, calibrate the subject's strength by trying to pull the subjects fingers apart.

3. Once you have calibrated the normal strength of the subject, the tester will ask the subject to say "yes" and will try to pull the subject's fingers apart. Repeat, this time asking the subject to say "no." Once the muscle response to "yes" and "no" is calibrated by the tester, you can start testing the beliefs listed below.

4. The tester will ask the subject to say one of the beliefs and will quickly try to pull the fingers apart. If the subject stays strong, it means she believes the statement to be true, and if she goes weak, she does not believe in the statement. If the fingers stay firmly together, the answer is yes, and if they come apart even a little, the answer is no.

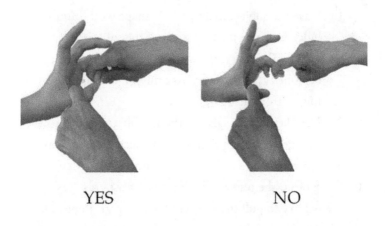

YES   NO

If you are on your own, here are two different ways to muscle test:

Solo Standing Method

1. Using a compass, determine which direction is north. Most smart phones have a compass app you can use.
2. Stand facing north with your spine erect, tall, and even.
3. Say "yes" and see what happens to your body. Most likely, your body will move forward slightly. Say "no," and your body will lean back slightly. For some people the polarity is reversed, so leaning forward is no and leaning backwards is yes. However, you can spend some time calibrating your muscle responses so you know what a "yes" and "no" feels like.
4. Now you are ready to test your beliefs.

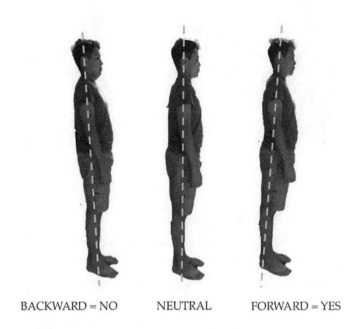

BACKWARD = NO   NEUTRAL   FORWARD = YES

Solo Finger Method

1. Make an "O" shape with your non-dominant hand using your thumb and ring finger.
2. Insert the thumb and index finger of your dominant hand into the O and spread the thumb and index fingers apart to break it.
3. Test "yes" and "no" repeating the process above.
4. Now you are ready to test your beliefs.

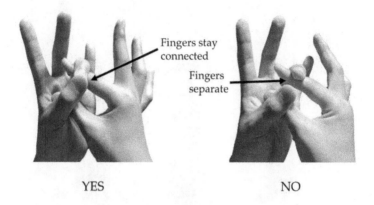

Fingers stay connected

Fingers separate

YES   NO

Caveats to Muscle Testing

If you do not get a response from your body, it may be that you are dehydrated. Muscles tighten when dehydrated, so make sure to drink plenty of water before testing.

I once worked with a client whose body did not respond to muscle testing. So instead of persisting, I decided to dig into her beliefs about her body. Through our conversation, I was able to ascertain that she believed her body to be sinful and not to be trusted. She was raised in a conservative Muslim family, where women's sexuality was considered evil. Despite her upbringing, she was strong in the fire element, and thus was a passionate and sexually active woman. Torn between her sensual desires and the conservative values of her family, she unconsciously believed her body to be sinful and thus not to be trusted. Once we cleared her limiting beliefs about her body, she was able to use muscle testing.

False Beliefs

We are all plagued by false beliefs, which become our inner demons that deplete us of energy, confidence and literally eat us up inside. Now that we have our lie detector set up, take a look at the following beliefs. For some of these, you won't even have to muscle test because your mind-body will react immediately as you say the statements out loud. Test all of them anyway. Sometimes your unconscious beliefs are sneaky and are well-hidden to our conscious mind.

I have created a list below of some general beliefs, as well as those most common for each element. However, test yourself for all of the following beliefs – even the ones that are not in your element. Since we are all made up of all the elements, it is possible to carry beliefs of elements that are not dominant in your constitution. Many of these beliefs may sound like they are saying the same things, but the brain is quite precise. Even a subtle shift of words will change your response to them.

Test to see if you hold any of these beliefs:

I know what love feels like.
I deserve love.
I love myself.
I accept myself.
I deserve pleasure.
I am enough.
Desiring pleasure is sinful.
I am unlucky in love.

I am unworthy of love.
I am unworthy of happiness.
Love needs to be earned.
I must be alone to be closer to God.
All good men are taken.
Love hurts.
My love always leaves me.
Being alone connects me to my family/lineage.
Being unlucky in love connects me to my family/lineage.
I have to sacrifice my love life for my children.
Nobody wants to be with a woman with so much baggage.
A man will take away time with my children.

When the seven elements are out of balance, these are some of the beliefs they may carry:

FIRE
Men are toys.
Passion is love.
Women are superior to men.
Passion is more important to me than commitment.

WATER
Love hurts.
It is safer to be alone.
Love is exhausting.
I will be abandoned if I love.

Breaking the Spell with Blessings

Our beliefs and programming are like a spell over us, perhaps even a curse. Yet we have the power within us to free ourselves.

Throughout history, blessings and prayers were ways humans connected to the divine. John Donahue, a master poet who wrote a beautiful book on blessings says, "a blessing is a not-sentiment or a question; it is gracious invocation where the human heart pleads with the divine heart." Through blessing and prayers we can break our spells. The process works as we connect to something that is greater than our own egos and stories. The blessing acknowledges our unlimited self and our birth-right and ability to connect to the infinite Creator.

ThetaHealing®, developed by Vianna Stibal, essentially uses the power of intention to connect to the Creative source of all that is to provide healing in the mind, body, and soul. We can all connect this source of healing with an ardent wish contained in blessing or prayer. Here is a sample script for a blessing/prayer. You may create your own that fits your personal belief system.

I, [insert your name], a child of the infinite Creator, give my soul in all its manifestations the power to transform my belief [insert your belief] in the highest and best way. Amen.

Once you identified the belief you would like to clear, close your eyes and take a few deep breaths. Scan your body from head to toe to see if you are holding any tension. After you say

EARTH

Love is unsafe.

I must be responsible to be loved.

I must sacrifice myself to be loved.

I will be disappointed if I desire love / happiness / pleasur

I will be disappointed if I desire happiness.

Men are superior to women.

AIR

Ignorance is bliss.

It is better to avoid pain than to face it.

I must keep my secrets to be loved.

My freedom is more important than love.

My freedom is more important than commitment.

METAL

I must be perfect to be loved.

I can do without love.

Intimacy is weakness.

WOOD

Love ties me down.

Love is boring.

SPIRIT

Romantic love is limiting

the blessing, take a moment to feel the energetic shift in your body. Keep your eyes closed for a few more minutes to feel the unfolding change in sensations in your body. It is important to *feel* the impact of the words you speak, as your physical sensations are bearing witness to and thus manifesting the shift in your beliefs.

Breath of Life to Heal and Transform

Your breath can be used not only be used to regulate emotions by directly influencing the autonomic nervous system, it can also be used to clear stagnate energy and heal past trauma trapped in your body.

It is said in the Bible that Adam, made of dust, came into being through a breath of life:

> *Then the Lord God formed a man from the dust of the ground and breathed into his nostrils the breath of life, and the man became a living being.*
> **-Genesis 2:7**

In esoteric traditions, this breath of life is known as Prana, Chi, or Spirit. Mystics and ancient sages knew that we are able to purify and energize ourselves with breath. Breath allows us to move the life force of the Creator in our bodies to heal us and transform us. On a scientific level, breath allows us to take in oxygen and expel carbon dioxide. It is also the only function we can consciously control that directly influences our autonomic nervous system. In other words, ancient sages and modern doctors agree that breath can transform fear and anxiety into peace and serenity.

EXERCISE: Transforming the Demon

We have said earlier that everything is alive. Your programming and beliefs are also alive, and are entities unto themselves. It is also true that what we resist persists. Instead of fighting your inner demons, you can use your awareness and breath to transform these negative entities into your allies. The following is a powerful exercise from Tibetan Bon Shamanic traditions to transform your inner demons.

This is a rather long meditation. You can go to my website at www.sukisohn.com/resources to download an audio version.

PREPARATION:

Find a comfortable seat and close your eyes to keep your awareness in your body. Once you are comfortably seated, pay attention to your breath. Scan your body to see where you hold any physical, emotional, and mental tension, and then breathe into that spot and release it with an exhale. Continue until you have released the tension you have identified with your breath.

STEP 1: MEETING THE DEMON

1. Identify your demon. A demon can be a fear, a belief, a feeling that is holding you back. It could even be a physical discomfort. It can be pretty much anything that is eating you up.

2. Recall an incident in your life when this demon came up.

3. Scan your body to feel where you're holding this demon and bring your attention to that place.

4. Materialize the demon: If it were to have a color, what color would it be? What shape does it take? What is its texture? What is its temperature? What does it smell like?

5. Intensify the image, and with your intention and an exhale, gently move or push the demon out of your body.

6. Now we are going to personify this demon. You see this demon taking shape with arms, legs, body, and head. What color is the demon? What gender is the demon? Notice its size. What is the density of its body? What is the surface of its body like? Notice the look in its eyes. What is the emotional state? What is its character like?

7. Now notice something about it you didn't notice before.

STEP 2: BECOMING THE DEMON

1. Now are going to ask this demon three questions:
   - What do you want?
   - What do you really need?
   - How will you feel if you get what you really need?

2. This next step may take a bit of courage. You are now going to go into the body of the demon. This demon is very real, but it also has always been a part of you. You are just now bringing it into the light of awareness. Become the demon.

3. Once you really feel being the demon, answer these questions:
   - What I want is……
   - What I really need is….
   - If I get what really need, I will feel….

STEP 3: FEEDING THE DEMON

1. Take a moment to come back into your own body and see the demon in front of you again.

2. Now imagine that your own body is dissolving into a beautiful radiant elixir. The quality of the elixir is the feeling the demon will get when it gets what it really needs.

3. Now, let the elixir flow to the demon.

4. See how the demon receives the elixir and is nurtured by it.

5. Notice how the demon receives it. Does it absorb it through its skin, is it poured over it, or is the demon drinking it?

6. Notice what happens to the demon. Notice if it's completely satisfied. If not, offer some more until it is completely satisfied. There is a limitless supply of this elixir.

7. When the demon is completely satisfied, notice what has happened to it. Has it morphed into another being? Has it disappeared?

STEP 4: MEETING THE ALLY

1. If it has morphed, ask, "Are you the ally?" and listen to the answer. If the demon says "no" (or if, when you fed the demon, it disappeared), we will now invite the ally to appear.

2. Now notice the details of the ally. What color is the ally? What gender is it? Notice its size. What is the density of its body? What is the surface of its body like? Notice the look in its eyes. What is its character like? Now notice something about it you didn't notice before.

3. Now we are going to ask the ally some questions:
   - How will you help me?
   - How will you protect me?
   - What pledge do you make to me?
   - How can I access you?

STEP 5: BECOMING THE ALLY

1. Again, you may encounter some resistance going into the body of your ally. But your ally has been with you all along. You are only now just becoming consciously aware of its existence. Now allow yourself to be in the body of the ally. Notice how that feels to be the size, the gender, the density, the quality of the ally. Notice

what your normal self looks like from the ally's point of view.

2. Really become the ally, and once you feel this sensation completely answer the questions:
    *   I will help you by…
    *   I will protect you by….
    *   My pledge to you is…
    *   You can access me by…

STEP 6: INTEGRATING WITH THE ALLY

1. Come back to your body.
2. See the ally in front of you, and now feel the energy of the ally streaming into every single cell of your being. Notice the color of the energy, this light that is streaming into you. Feel it viscerally.
3. Now see that the ally is dissolving into light. That light dissolves into you, and as the light enters you, it is washing every part of you. From your toes, legs, chest, hands, arms, and head.
4. Notice what it feels like. And now simply rest in what is present after the dissolution.
5. Keeping awareness of the ally in your body, open your eyes and look around you. Notice if your surrounding look or feel different.
6. Now take a moment to journal your experience and the insights you have gained.

CHAPTER 6

Navigate and Nourish Your Body

"You only have to let the soft animal of your body love what it loves."
-MARY OLIVER

Many of us fail to connect to the inherent wisdom in the body. We are overly focused on our mental capacities, and have lost touch with the intuitive, mysterious, and powerful abilities of our bodies. In this chapter, we explore how the body works with regards to love and desire, and how to reclaim femininity through the body.

Pain and pleasure is felt in the body, whether the source of it is physical, emotional, or mental. Experience without the body is not possible. Imagine if you knew you were supposed to be experiencing heartbreak, but felt nothing in your body. Sociopaths are a bit like this. They have the mental notion that they should be *feeling* something, but they do not.

Take a look at the thermal diagram of human emotions below. As you can see, body temperatures vary depending on the emotions being experienced. Emotions are not a mental concept, but a felt sensation in the body.

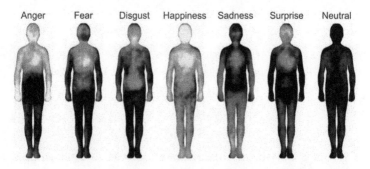

Figure 2: Thermal Imaging of Human Emotions,
Source: Tarlach, Gemma. "Body Atlas Reveals Where We Feel
Happiness and Shame."
From discovermagazine.com

Chakras & The Three Brains

Emotions are energy (or life force) in motion. Many ancient healing traditions understood that there are key energy centers in the body. There are seven major energy centers in the body, which the Indian Vedic traditions named chakras,. They correspond to important glands in the nervous system as well as to the seven elements.

ENERGY CENTER & QUALITY

HUMAN ORGAN & FUNCTION

Crown: Transcendence — **Pineal:** Circadian Rhtyhm

Third Eye: Vision — **Pituitary:** Master Gland

Throat: Expression — **Thyroid:** Metabolism

Heart: Connection — **Thymus:** Immune System

Solar Plexus: Personal Power — **Adrenals:** Energy

Sacral: Passion — **Gonads:** Sexual Functions

Root: Stability

Figure 3: Chakras and the Endocrine System

It is fascinating to see how the chakra system has a precise correspondence to the endocrine system. This may not be apparent at first, but if you take a closer look at the hormones secreted by each of the glands, you will see how the functions of these neurotransmitters relate to each chakra. Here I will discuss three chakras in particular.

The Taoists believed that chakras were divided into two types – "gates" and "palaces." The gates are the first, third, fifth, and seventh chakras. The first chakra, at the base of body, is how we physically came into this world. The third is a gate to self-empowerment, the fifth is a gate to the metaphysical realm, and the seventh a gate to the divine world.

The palaces were considered to be places where energy can be cultivated and stored. The palaces are the second chakra (the womb and gut), the fourth chakra (the heart and middle palace), and the sixth chakra (the brain and the upper palace). If you would like to learn more about the chakra systems, Anodea Judith's book *Eastern Body Western Mind* and *Healing Chakra* by Ilchi Lee are excellent resources. Each palace has an intelligence and function of its own. This is not a book about chakras, so I will not go into too much detail about the qualities of each, but we will further explore recent scientific studies done on these three palaces and their effects on our emotions and behavior.

Scientists are now discovering that we have not one but *three* brains – head brain, heart brain, and gut brain (Soosalu, *mBraining*). Our gut and heart brains play an integral part in our emotions and behavior. The gut is the primary producer of dopamine which, when released, is experienced as desire, motivation, and pleasure. Neuroscientist, Vaughn Bell, described it as the Kim Kardashian of neurotransmitters. Do you remember a time when you were madly in love and so full with thoughts of your beloved that you didn't feel hungry? Well, that's dopamine for you. Dopamine is also the chemical most related to addictions. It is the high we experience from the release of dopamine that gets us hooked on something (or someone). The gut is also linked to our sense of identity, and closely linked to security and survival. When we feel betrayed or threatened we feel it in our gut. Our instincts are felt in our gut, too. Our gut brain is linked to our reptilian brain, the oldest part of our brain and linked to functions of survival.

Across centuries and cultures, the heart was considered the source of emotion, wisdom, courage, and connection. Emotions of love – both good and bad – are felt in the heart, hence the word heartache. Research has shown that the heart communicates to the brain in four major ways: neurologically (through the transmission of nerve impulses), biochemically (through hormones and neurotransmitters), biophysically (through pressure waves), and energetically (through electromagnetic field interactions) (McCraty, *Science of the Heart*). Communication along all these conduits significantly affects the brain's activity. Biochemically, the heart produces at least half of our supply of oxytocin. This neurotransmitter is commonly known as the love or social bonding hormone. This hormone is released in copious amounts following childbirth to ensure a mother's attachment to her newborn baby. Oxytocin is also released in the presence of, or even in thoughts of, our lovers. The thymus gland, which controls our immune system, is also located near the heart. Our immune system is what dictates whether a foreign cell is considered to be friend or foe (Soosalu, *mBraining*). Much like the heart, which determines who we will repel or bond with.

Above all, the most fascinating aspect of the heart is its ability to bio-magnetically communicate between people. Scientists have found that there is a direct relationship between the heart-rhythm patterns and the metaphysical information encoded in the magnetic field radiated by the heart (McCraty, *Science of the Heart*). Not only that, but in close proximity, individuals often synchronize their heart-rhythms. When we talk about good vibes, we are sensing this electromagnetic field of another person. Some individuals are particularly sensitive to this kind of bio-electromagnetic signals (McCraty, *Science of the Heart*). These individuals are naturally more empathic and intuitive. In other words, the heart is the source of love, bonding and empathy.

The heart brain determines the *why*, i.e., the purpose of any decision, and that's why the heart must lead the way. The gut brain provides the motivation and drive to take action, while the head brain figures out the best way to achieve the desired outcome. In our search for love, we mistakenly lead with the head. Our mental check list for Mr. Right is one example of leading with the head. This is like putting a technician in the position of a CEO. Your brain is simply not equipped to handle these kind of decisions. Sages across the world have been promoting heart-centered life for centuries. Lead with the heart, trust your gut, so that you can "let the soft animal of your body love what it loves…"

Healing the Heart and Soul through the Body

In his book *Waking the Tiger: Healing the Trauma,* renowned trauma specialist Peter Levine says that the body has the instinctual capacity to heal:

> *Body sensation, rather than intense emotion, is the key to healing trauma... What we need to do to be freed from our symptoms and fears is arouse our deep physiological resources and consciously utilize them. If we remain ignorant of our power to change the course of our instinctual responses in a proactive rather than reactive way, we will continue being imprisoned by them... Sensations come from symptoms, and symptoms come from compressed energy; that energy is what we have to work with in this process. Through sensation and the felt sense, the vast energy can gradually be decompressed and harnessed for the purpose of transforming trauma.*

Levine discusses how animals in the wild are repeatedly subject to traumatic circumstances – such as being hunted by a predator – yet emerge from the experience psychologically unscathed. Upon narrowly escaping a predator, an impala's first reaction is to violently shake its body. According to Levine, through this action, the impala is able to *literally* shake off the trauma.

Throughout this book I introduce several exercises that bring your awareness to the negative emotions and trauma trapped in your body. *Brain Wave Vibration* and *Dancing Your Way to*

Femininity are some exercises that I have presented in this book. I have also included the exercise *Transforming the Inner Demons* to use body sensations to identify the negative emotions and use intention to transform these negative emotions into an ally.

There is nothing that is intrinsically evil or negative in the world. It is rather limited human perspective that is patterned to see the world as good and evil. By shifting, moving, and transforming energy as it is felt in our bodies, we are able to free ourselves from the limited view of the world that brings much suffering to our lives.

Listening to the Body

I hear some women say, "I have made too many mistakes and I can't trust my judgement anymore." Well, here are some practical guidelines on how to tap into the intuitive power of your body, so you can learn to trust yourself again. Muscle testing is used by many alternative healers such as kinesiologists and nutritionists to determine the source and prescription for our ailments. Our body instinctively knows what is good for us. Here, I am not talking about desires of hunger and lust for instant gratification that people often mistake as the body. Rather, we are talking about the body that stores infinite amount of unfiltered sensory data in its billions of cells.

You can use muscle testing to make many decisions, provided that you frame your questions correctly. The deepest wisdom comes from within you, and it can be tapped into by learning how to correctly listen to your body.

As I mentioned earlier, leading with the head, especially when it comes to romantic love, is a bad idea. This is what leading with the head sounds like: "I was married for ten years to a good person who tried very hard to be a good husband. He was loyal, honest, dependable, and funny. I loved him in large part because I felt like he was the kind of guy I should marry. And I bent over backward to be the good wife." When you are saying you *should* love someone, that is your head brain talking. It's based on logic and reason. But if your heart is not on board, the relationship will likely not last, or you won't feel a heartfelt fulfillment and simply go through the motions. Besides, don't you think it's unfair for you to deprive this "honest, dependable, good man" from having a genuinely loving relationship?

Just as troublesome is leading with your gut brain. Your gut brain is related to pleasure, desire, and security. It's always looking for that hit of dopamine. My client Maria was a case in point. Instead of seeking true intimate relationships leading with the heart, she was unconsciously looking for a quick fix with her sexual escapades, hoping that it would lead to a long-term romantic relationship.

So then, what does leading with the heart feel like? It is like a beautiful spring day, where you feel the subtle warmth spread from your heart to your body. We often mistake passion and lust for love. Passion you will most likely feel from the lower abdomen spreading as a rush of heat to your head and limbs. It feels more like a hot summer day. There is nothing wrong with passion, but leading with it, without the heart's bonding, will most likely result in a short-lived romance. We are simply wired that way.

I learned from a Kabbalist the importance of restriction for long term gain. The Law of Resistance states that there is light and energy all around us. Like electricity, it is not good or bad in its original nature, but how this light energy manifests in our lives is determined by how we receive it. A direct injection without any resistance results in momentary but electrifying jolt of pleasure. We must practice restriction to create resistance in order to maintain a constant flow of light and energy into our lives. He used a light bulb as an analogy. The way a light bulb works is that electricity flows through a thin wire in the light bulb called the filament. The filament used in a bulb has a property called "resistance." The resistance is the amount of friction that an object will put against electricity flowing through it. The resistance to electric current is what creates heat and light. The greater the resistance, the brighter and hotter the light.

Applied to humans, resistance can be translated to restriction. Your gut brain might be wanting to satisfy your physical urges by jumping to this hot new guy you just met, but restriction is what will keep the flame going. If the filament is unable to do its job, the two poles come together and give off a momentarily bright light before it explodes – this is what we call a short circuit. A short circuit is like a hot one night stand: intense and seductive at the time, but unlikely to last.

In fact, Kabbalist recommend a tool which they call *Purity of the Family* to keep passion alive in a long-term committed relationship. The basic premise of the tool is to increase desire by restricting touch, any kind of touch, during the period of menstruation and the following seven days. This restriction creates appreciation for intimate touch that is often taken for granted in long-term relationships.

Your head and gut may try to dissuade you from your heart's decision, and it is important that your heart, head, and gut stay aligned. Your heart should take heed of its trusted advisors, the brain and gut. But, like the CEO of a company, the buck stops at the heart.

EXERCISE: Aligning the Heart, Head, and Gut

Your head and gut may try to dissuade you from your heart's decision, and it is important that your heart, head, and gut stay aligned. Your heart should take heed of its trusted advisors, the brain and gut. But, like the CEO of a company, the buck stops at the heart.

Here is a simple exercise you can do when you are in doubt to bring your heart, head, and gut into alignment.

1. Pick a problem or issue that you feel confused about. Throughout the exercise, pay close attention to the physical sensations in your body.
2. Close your eyes, take a few deep breaths.

3. Now bring your attention to your heart. Notice what physical sensations there are in your heart. Does it feel tight or expansive? Does it feel warm and tingly, or tight and rigid?

4. When you are feeling completely present in your heart, ask your heart, "What do you truly want?" and wait for an answer. Pay close attention to stirrings in your heart.

5. It may take a minute or so, but be patient and continue to be present in your heart. Don't second-guess yourself or dismiss what you hear as an overactive imagination.

6. Once your heart has shared its truths, time for the head and gut to have their say.

7. Shift your attention to your abdomen. What sensations do you feel in your gut? Is it relaxed and comfortable or tight and knotted?

8. Paying attention to the sensations you feel in your gut, ask your question. "How do you feel about the Heart's desire?"

9. Finally, bring your attention to your head. Notice what sensations are there.

10. Can you feel your left and right hemispheres equally or does it feel like one side is lit up while the other side feels "absent"? Does it feel tense and heated, or cool and expansive?

11. While connected to these sensations, ask your head, "What do you think about the Heart's desire? How can you support the Heart's desire?"

12. When you are done, take a moment to write down what your three brains have shared.

Redefining and Reclaiming Femininity

I often hear that they simply don't feel sexy or feminine anymore. For professional working moms in corporate jobs it's a double whammy, as it is very likely that her supposedly masculine aspect is encouraged and rewarded more readily at work. What I find interesting is women's view on femininity. When asked "What is feminine?" somebody will frequently answer with words like soft, gentle, yielding, passive, nurturing, sensitive, emotional, and sensual. Masculine traits, on the other hand, are typically defined as strong, forward, active, direct, logical, stable, and disciplined.

However, when it comes to being a mother, most women will agree that she is an equal balance of these so-called "feminine" and "masculine" traits. What could be more feminine than being a mother? In the past, in many cultures the matriarch managed all the finances of the house, as well as managing the household staff. When has the feminine solely been identified with meek and yielding? Femininity can be powerful, direct, and fierce.

What I sense that these women mean when they say they don't feel feminine is that they do not feel *sensual*. Modern society's extreme focus on intellectual capabilities of the head brain all but disconnect us from our bodies. I meet many women lacking in any type of body awareness, and as a result they have a stiff awkwardness in their movement. I find that body practices such as dancing and Tai Chi are helpful in reconnecting women to their bodies. What about yoga, you say? Though I am a huge fan of yoga to increase strength and flexibility, the forms of yoga that have become most popular, i.e. power and hot yoga, do little to connect to fluidity of movement that is caused by subtle energy and vibrations. I would recommend Kundalini yoga or Body & Brain Yoga® for those who would like to incorporate a yoga practice to connect to their fluid feminine aspect.

Dana was a successful HR executive. She was an avid runner and had completed several marathons abroad. She also practiced yoga and went to the gym regularly. However, there was a persistent rigidity in her movement. I recommended that she start taking a warm bath with candle lights and spend at least an hour dancing once a week. After a couple of weeks, she came to me glowing and said that her lover had said, "Whatever you are doing, keep doing it!" Dana confessed that she felt more feminine and seductive as she reconnected to her body with these simple rituals.

Nature's Cycle and Femininity

Another unfortunate modern phenomenon that affects our relation to femininity is our disconnection to nature's rhythms. During a time when humans were more susceptible to the vagaries of nature, we respected and honored nature's cycles and were aware of these very cycles in women's bodies. As such, in traditional indigenous cultures, women were honored as life givers.

Menstrual blood was considered sacred and was offered to earth with prayers for a fertile and bountiful harvest from the earth. In traditional societies, women were allowed a time of rest during her cycle allowing for her to honor and respect the cycle of death and rebirth happening within her body. Nowadays, these monthly cycles are considered a nuisance rather than anything to be honored and appreciated.

As modern conveniences allowed us to be sheltered and protected, we have also lost the ability to sense nature's impact on our bodies. Our circadian rhythm, which controls our sleep cycle, is naturally regulated by the sun's light. But now with modern devices giving off blue light mimicking daylight, our sleep cycles have been thrown off, resulting in widespread insomnia.

Driven by our ambitions to achieve and our often misguided pursuit of perfection, we push our bodies with little consideration or awareness of our natural cycles. Though I am a big believer in consistency, discipline, and pushing one's boundaries, a lack of awareness of the body's cycles will only hurt us in the long run.

In America, when it comes to fitness regimes, like career and financial success, more is better. Ultimate fitness is defined by a lean and muscular physique achieved through long and intense hours in the gym. For many, the idea of replacing CrossFit workouts or marathon training programs with more gentle forms of exercise like Tai Chi or Qigong would be close to sacrilege, boring, or just a plain waste of time. But what is the true cost of this intensity?

According to Taoist philosophy, the Yin and Yang need to be balanced in a body, and excess of either throws us off physically, emotionally, and spiritually. Yang is hot. Yang burns energy. Yang consumes. In the right dose, it can be wonderful – promoting inspiration, movement, and vitality. But without the balance of Yin, Yang can become explosive. With excess Yang, we become restless, easily affected, irritable, aggressive, snappy, and even angry. Anxiety and insomnia are also common symptoms of excess Yang. Physically, when we use Yang/Energy to burn through our Yin/Resources too quickly, we are actually speeding up the aging process. Type-A personalities, common among metal and wood elements, are easily susceptible to excess of this nature, and as result they frequently suffer from emotional imbalances and chronic stress to the body brought on in the name of fitness.

True femininity respects the balance of Yin and Yang, as well as natural cycles of our body and nature. So reclaim your femininity by connecting to your body. Befriend your body and get to know what helps you to feel more harmonious and in flow.

Keep a consistent ritual to honor your femininity so that she can honor you with her presence in your life.

EXERCISE: Dance Your Way to Fluidity and Sensuality

Throughout human history, dance has been part of celebration, ceremony, rituals, and entertainment. A rigid mind creates a rigid body and vice versa. Dance is a tool of social interaction that promoted cooperation essential for survival for our ancestors. In ceremony and rituals, dance has been used to heal as well as chase away negative entities. By dancing, we are able to shift energy so that we can break through physical, emotional, and mental stagnancies. Gabrielle Roth, founder of Five Rhythms, a moving meditation movement said, "When the body moves, the mind stills."

Dancing is indeed one of the fastest and simplest ways to connect to your body and sensual femininity. I have prepared a couple of public playlists on Spotify. You can find the links to these at my website: www.sukisohn.com/resources. Each playlist is about 40 minutes long.

1. Once you have the music ready, take a moment to let the music soak into your body. Let the music infuse every cell in your body with its rhythm and melody.
2. Once you can feel the music vibrating in your cells, let the music move your body.
3. Surrender to the melody and beats and start to notice where there is stiffness or resistance both physically, emotionally, and mentally. Pay attention to every nook and cranny of your body by scanning it from head to toe.

4. See if you can release the tension you feel in the various parts of your body with movement. See what your body naturally wants to do to release the tension and surrender to it. Let it happen.

5. It is very likely that you may feel awkward and embarrassed even though nobody is watching. Just let it be, and continue to move to the music.

6. When the session is over, journal on what came up for you. Did you feel in flow, or did it feel awkward? What thoughts and feelings were going through your mind and body? Were you able to identify and release tension in different parts of your body?

7. Continue this practice regularly at least once a week until you feel completely comfortable and natural moving to music.

PART II

Relating to the Beloved

CHAPTER 7
Edify & Elucidate Yourself

How do you talk to a man so you can be heard? What are the differences in how men and women communicate? And how do you move forward from an initial attraction to a committed relationship? Men desire love, connection, and commitment just as much as women do, but how they express it and what drives them to do so is different.

Men Are Not Hairy Women

Besides the obvious physical differences, there are many clear distinctions between a male and female brain.

The brain is made up of white and grey matter. Grey matter areas are localized and are responsible for information and action processing. When these areas are activated it results in tunnel vision like focus. Once deeply engaged in a task in this state, individuals will not show much awareness or sensitivity to other people or their environment. White matter on the other hand is the brain's networking grid that connects the grey matter with other processing centers, which allow for transition to other thoughts, connections, as well as a broader perspective (Jantz, "Brain Differences Between Genders").

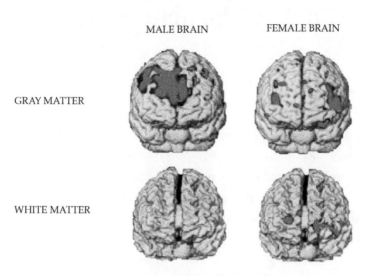

Figure 4: Gray and White Matter Difference in Male and Female Brain

Male brains engage seven times more gray matter for activity while the female brain uses ten times more white matter. The difference in utilization of white and gray matter have of course evolved over time to make us more efficient to our given roles as hunters and gatherers. Men who developed sharp focus to track prey or follow an enemy's movement during battle would have most likely been able to survive. While females, as primary caretakers of the children and the home, would have had to be able to shift their attention quickly, making sure the fire stayed lit ensuring there were no predators nearby to harm their young (Jantz, "Brain Differences Between Genders").

Biochemically, men process more testosterone (neurotransmitter that motivates us towards aggression and sex) while women process more estrogen (reproductive chemical) and oxytocin (bonding chemical). Structurally, female brains have verbal centers on both sides of the brain, while males tend to have verbal centers on only the left hemisphere. Women will tend to use more words engaging both sides of the brains, while men not only have fewer verbal centers in general but also, often, have less connectivity between their word centers and their memories or feelings. So when it comes to discussing feelings and emotions, men have a much harder time expressing themselves (Jantz, "Brain Differences Between Genders").

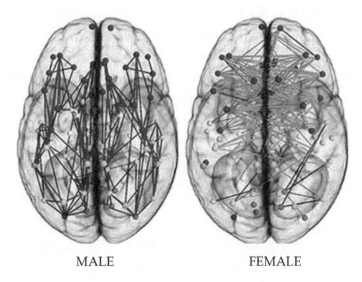

MALE   FEMALE

Figure 5: Communication Network in Male and Female Brain

All of this is to say, when you are feeling hurt by a perceived insensitivity of your man, don't take it personally. Getting a man to speak about his feelings when he is not ready to do so will only stir up resistance to the conversation and potentially to you. Though many men will be less willing and able to discuss their emotions than women, they are still receiving hormones and electromagnetic signals. In other words, they are picking up on your vibe, though they may not be consciously aware of it. Just as important as your words is the subtle energy that passes between you. How aware are you of the kind of vibe you are giving off? Are you needy, pouty, and resentful, or compassionate, patient, and open? Next time you have to have that all-important chat that involves the emotions, observe what kind of vibe you are bringing to the conversation.

Don't Make Him Guess

While the female brain, with its extensive white matter network, is able to make connections and infer, the male brain is compartmentalized. Women are often disappointed when their lovers can't sense that they are upset or guess what their needs are, because to them the signals are obvious! However, to a man it's a complete mystery. Next time your beloved can't guess or understand your feelings, bring it up with God, not your man. Since it's unlikely that you will get God to change the structure of man's brain instantaneously, why not shift your tactics to get the outcome you want? Clearly state your needs in a factual manner so that your man's brain can process it. Remember, it's not that he is insensitive, he just does not have the network of white matter that allows him to guess your needs.

Respect vs. Love

For most women, attention and affection means love, but to a man, respect means love. Men's brains aren't wired for the touchy-feely stuff. Nor is this kind of behavior encouraged by his peers or society at large. Both biology and social conditioning steer men away from expressing their feelings, while moving them towards achievement and action. Ask any man around you what they would pick if they had to choose between love or respect from their long-term life partners – most men will choose respect. There is nothing more emasculating for a man than to feel disrespected by their partner. When a man feels emasculated, he will most likely shut down and push you away – if not physically, at least emotionally. On the flip side, if your love makes him feel like Superman, he will be putty in your hands.

Freedom & Men

Men have an innate biological desire to be free. The male intimacy and sexuality expert David Deida says, "The masculine is always seeking release from constraint into freedom. The feminine often doesn't understand these masculine ways and needs." How are we as women to work with our man's inherent need for freedom?

While God in her infinite wisdom made men seek freedom, she made a woman's natural state one of flow and change. Throughout our lives, we transform from maid, to mother, to crone. Our bodies change every month and throughout the years. Our natural state is very much like the moon and the ocean tides. Just as how when the sun gazes at the moon with its steadfast rays, she changes her shape constantly, a woman is capable of transforming herself constantly. She can do this while completely staying true to who she is, just as the moon does.

Fully embrace the feminine essence of change, and you can delightedly watch how the masculine is pleasantly surprised, intrigued, and sometimes puzzled. A woman's fluidity, at its core, allows a man to experience freedom within commitment. That old adage that a woman must be a lady in the living room, a gourmand in the kitchen, and a seductress in the bedroom isn't far from the truth. You may balk at this if you are fixed in your ways and unwilling to embrace the constant metamorphosis that is the birthright of women.

How to Speak to Men So You Will Be Heard

Men are not just hairy women, so engaging your man the way you do your best girlfriend and expecting him to respond the way she does is not a realistic expectation. As mentioned above, women's brains draw from both hemispheres fluidly when verbally expressing, while men more likely stick to their compartmentalized gray matter pockets. This means that women tend to use many more words in their communication. Just because he is not interested in every little detail you have to say does not mean he does not care for you. It's simply that all that detail makes his head spin! Next time you are on a date or when you need to speak to your man about something important, keep your communication style simple and direct, with less unnecessary detail. This does not mean you can't be affectionate, creative, or artistic in how you communicate – just lose the superlatives. Also, it is important to recognize and know when your man is not available, and it would be wise not to force the issue at those times.

What if it's never the right time for him? There are three possibilities to consider if you feel stonewalled by your man.

1. Have you clearly expressed your need in a matter-of-fact manner, free of superlatives and emotion?
2. Are you forcing him to guess what your needs are when he really just doesn't get it?

3. In what frame of mind are you reaching out to him?
    Is it filled with a need for validation and desperation?
    Are you being overly emotional?

This leads us to our next topic of neediness.

Caution Against Neediness

Apart from poor hygiene, nothing is a bigger turn off than neediness. When you do not feel whole and are looking for someone to fill a void in you, it can result in desperation, baseless jealousy, obsession, and addiction. If you are looking for someone else to validate that you are loveable, desirable, and worthy, you will always be disappointed.

My client Nancy was divorced twice, and even before her second divorce paperwork was filed, she was already looking for her next relationship. She had just met James, who was a bohemian traveler type who never stuck to a long-term job or location. She was fixated on him, as she felt he was everything she wanted to be – free. After a couple of dates, he started ghosting her, which sent her into a downward spiral of negativity. She berated herself for not being attractive or feminine enough. She believed she was too heavy, too boring, and basically unworthy of love.

She also felt that she was living out her family's legacy. She was of Middle Eastern descent and was raised in a patriarchal and conservative household. Her grandmother was abused and abandoned by her husband. Her mother divorced her alcoholic and physically abusive husband only to die of breast cancer shortly after. Tragedy and bad luck with men ran in her family. This made her more desperate to make it work with a man.

No wonder she couldn't make a relationship work. The more she clung to the story of being rescued from herself and her lineage by a man, the more desperate she became.

I asked her how she would feel about taking a break from the idea of dating and meeting a man. I recommended that she take at least a year to spend time with herself and get comfortable with her own company. She agreed. The next session, she came in glowing and happy without a trace of desperation. She said, "The moment I decided to take on this dating fast, men started coming out of the woodworks. Even James started reaching out again." The moment she drew back her desperation and clawing attitude, men started moving towards her. Sometimes you have to create space and time for a man to reach out. We will discuss this in more detail in Chapter 8: Tempt and Tease Yourself into His Heart.

Understand his Patterns

Having no brothers or male cousins around when I was growing up, I was surprised to learn how sensitive boys are when I had my first son. Of course, society and peers attempt to beat that sensitivity out of them at an early age, but raising my own two boys gave me invaluable insight into the male psyche. Men are sensitive and vulnerable, too! However, since the admission and expression of their vulnerability is less socially acceptable, they channel it into aggression, withdrawal, and sometimes both.

When a man gets passed on for an important promotion, or he is sexually frustrated, or he is about to launch a big new project and is feeling a little apprehensive, he will most likely express himself in the same way – withdrawn grouchiness. (Of course, some men will become belligerent and physically or emotionally abusive when slighted. If this is the case for you, I would advise that you get out of dating this man as soon as possible. He obviously needs to do a lot more work on his own before he is civilized enough to be in a caring relationship.)

If you ask a man if anything is wrong, he will most likely say, "I'm fine." I find that trying to get my teenage son to talk about his day is not all that different from trying to get my husband to tell me what is bothering him. Men feel that they need to fix their own problems, and talking it out is not something that they will immediately resort to, especially to the women in their lives.

So it's a good thing women have more white matter to make connections. Learn your man's patterns with the objectivity of a scientist. Do not make it about you and let your emotions rob you of your intelligence. Find out what triggers make your man withdraw. In many cases, there is a very simple reason, like he had a rough day at work or his bike broke down. You don't need to do anything about these things – unless of course the problem involves you, like sex. Just give him the space and trust that he will work things out on his own or he will reach out when he is ready.

Never Fake Who You Are but Be Willing to Change Everything

We often become more resistant and sometimes even uncomfortable with change as we age. That is why many people believe it's harder to meet a romantic partner when you are older. On the flip side, our age has helped shape a clear sense of identity and personal boundaries. And if you are reading this book and got this far, there is clearly something you want to change in your life. We need to engage romantic relationships with truthfulness, but also with a willingness to change everything.

My client Laura was a successful corporate lawyer in in her mid-forties. She raised her kids on her own after her husband passed away from a sudden heart attack several years back. Now that her children were off to college, she more keenly felt her loneliness and was looking for a relationship. However, she had a rigid daily routine and a corresponding mentality that didn't allow space, literally and figuratively, for a relationship. Between her frequent travels, busy work schedule, and daily spinning class, she didn't have a free hour in her day for idle downtime. She unconsciously filled her time so that she would not have idle time to feel lonely.

Then she had a minor injury that forced her to pull back from her demanding work schedule and gym time. This involuntary downtime allowed her to re-examine her priorities. She realized that while she claimed to want a romantic relationship, she was clearly sending a message to the universe that she didn't have room for one. Her injury was a turning point for Laura, who not only shifted her schedule, but became visibly softer and more relaxed. She started exploring new hobbies and interests, and started utilizing online dating apps to meet men.

She had not dated since she was in her twenties, and all of the new dating apps seemed alien. Swiping left or right to choose a candidate seemed downright distasteful. But she persisted, embraced the new technology, and she met someone quite unexpectedly.

Her new love interest, Tony, was several years her junior and had never been married or had kids. At first, she was apprehensive. He was so different from her ex-husband, who was also a lawyer. Tony was a travel writer who frequently spent extended periods of time in the most remote places on earth. During one of his trips, he invited her to join him. She hesitantly agreed, then immediately fell in love with the exotic and open landscape of the wild, to her surprise. After having lived her entire adult life in large cities, cooped up in glass buildings under fluorescent lights, she finally felt alive. She decided to quit her job and accompany Tony on trips for a while. They eventually decided to work together, and started a company to organize specialized tours to these beautiful remote locations.

One thing that is guaranteed never to change is change itself. Instead of resisting the inevitable, open yourself, mind and heart, to a new adventure that may await you.

Be the Sanctuary Your Man Seeks

Men live in a competitive world. You may argue that women do too in their professional lives, but our interactions are naturally based on collaboration rather than establishing a pecking order. At work or in social situations, men exhibit the mentalities of pack animals, where they are constantly posturing to gain more status in their groups. Women, on the other hand, reach out to their peers for support and comfort. The fact that men process more testosterone, the neurotransmitter for aggression and sexual drive, while women process more oxytocin, the chemical for bonding, underlies the natural inclinations of how women and men relate to their social communities.

Men want a sanctuary where they can rest and recharge in the face of another day of "battle," and they want that place to be in your arms. How able are you to become the sanctuary for your man? Can you put aside your own anxieties and frustrations with no agenda and hold space for your beloved in compassion? It is an obvious and simple request, yet not easy to fulfill. Metal types who are always vigilant will find this to be the most difficult among the elements because they don't know what a sanctuary feels like.

You certainly won't be able to become a sanctuary for another if you can't be one for yourself. How able are you to inspire and encourage yourself when you feel discouraged or exhausted? Develop consistent nurturing rituals like dancing, massage, warm baths, or meditation. Find what helps you get to a place of serenity and compassion so that you may be able to extend the same to others.

At the end of the day, your ability to be sensual, fluid, confident, and insightful comes from your choice to be those things. Once you make that choice from the deepest part of your heart, your brain will figure out how and your gut will give you the energy and drive to make it happen.

Make Resolving Conflict Fun

Having a sense of humor and playfulness is critical for a healthy relationship.

My husband and I have a game called the "Snap Jar". No matter how hard you try to be kind and compassionate to your partner, there will be days where this gets very challenging. Whether it is a lack of sleep due to a new born baby or stress at work, when we are low on energy, we have little to give and tend to snap at our partners out of anger and irritability. The Snap Jar is a little bet that we have going to discourage snapping at each other. When either one of snaps at each other, we agreed to put $20 into the Snap Jar. This simple bet with each other introduces levity and humor during stressful times so that we can prevent going down a vicious cycle of reactive behavior.

Another tool that I introduce to clients is the Safe Sign. It is a simple hand gesture that couple agrees on to use when a conversation gets too heated and unproductive. Either party can use the hand gesture at any time to stop the conversation instantly to allow space to revisit the issue another time.

Be proactive about conflict. If you find a negative pattern developing in your relationship, put your heads together to come up with a creative and playful way to resolve the conflict.

CHAPTER 8

Tempt & Tease Your Way into His Heart

"Nothing makes a woman more beautiful than the belief that she is beautiful."
-Sophia Loren

Why are we attracted to some people and repelled by others? There are a number of obvious factors like looks, personality, interests, and values, but there are many more invisible variables that influence our decisions, as well.

The Science of Human Attraction

Foremost, there are biological factors that influence attraction. According to some scientists, smell is one of the most important determinants. In one study, scientists found that women were able to smell how symmetrical a man's features are based on smell only and used that information to judge attractiveness (Boltzman, "Study Finds Signs of Elusive Pheromones in Human").

I once had a client who dated a wonderful man who was attractive, intelligent, interesting, and kind. They had many similar interests and many friends in common. On the surface, he really checked off all the boxes for Mr. Right. But the moment he leaned in close, she immediately felt repelled by him. It wasn't body odor. It was his natural scent that repelled her.

No matter how hard she tried to like him, she couldn't get over his smell. His pheromones just didn't quite work for her. There of course was a complex array of biological markers that made him incompatible for her, so no matter how much her rational mind thought he was a good suitor, her body rejected him.

Trust your nose. It knows stuff that your conscious mind does not.

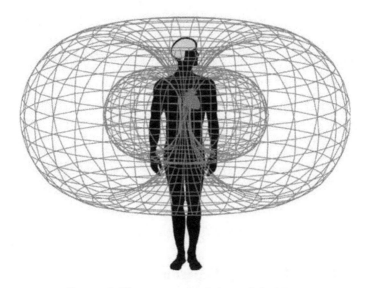

Figure 6: Electromagnetic Sphere of the Heart
Source: Heart Math Institute.

I have discussed earlier that the heart emits a bio-electromagnetic signal. The range of this sphere reaches about 7 feet around us and potentially farther with focused intention or strong emotions (McCraty, *Science of the Heart*). When you are around someone who is extremely angry, it is easy pick up on that energy even if that person is trying not to show it. You unconsciously will try to avoid this person, especially if you are not in an angry state yourself.

It is a law of physics that when two different frequencies collide, they will eventually synchronize. You can see this when you drop two pebbles in a pond. At first the two pebbles create distinct ripple patterns, but after the two patterns meet they start to merge, creating one large concentric pattern. It works the same way with the electromagnetic signals we send out from our hearts towards others. This is why negativity begets negativity. But unlike pebbles dropped into a pond, we have free will – and two feet. We can walk away from frequencies that do not make us feel good. Einstein said:

Everything is energy and that's all there is to it. Match the frequency of the reality you want and you cannot help but get that reality. It can be no other way. This is not philosophy. This is physics!

EXERCISE: Energy Experiment

The concept of energy and even "vibes" is becoming more mainstream, but I would love for you to have a first-hand experience of your energy and your ability to harness and move it.

1. Take a comfortable seat with your back straight. Place your hands on your thighs with palms facing up. Take a few deep breaths.
2. With your next inhale, float your palms up so that they are facing each other in front of your heart but not touching. Exhale. Bring your attention to the center of your palms.
3. With your next inhale, expand the space between your palms, and with your exhale contract the space between them.
4. Bring your focus to your palms and pay attention to the sensation you feel. You may feel a tingling, a

warmth, or even a gentle push and pull sensation as you expand and contract your palms with your breath.

5. Now focus on the magnetic push and pull sensation between your palms.

6. Once you feel this sensation strongly, keep your left palm where it is while moving your right palm out. With your attention focusing on the magnetic sensation, push your right palm out, and then reverse the polarity and pull your palm back towards the other palm.

Your hands are one of the most sensitive parts of your body, which is why this training starts with your hands. You can, however, extend the energetic sensation throughout your body. You can literally attract and repel people from you with your intention. In fact, we are all already doing this – but unconsciously.

Mind Your Vibes

Whether you are aware of this or not, you are constantly emitting signals about what is in your heart to those around you. Kindness, compassion, patience, sincerity, joy, or love in one person can be felt by another person without exchanging a single word. The same way desperation, negativity, bitterness, suspicion, anger, or jealousy can be felt. Most healthy individuals will naturally want to withdraw from this kind of person. If you ever wonder, "Why do I keep on attracting the same kind of a-hole?", ask yourself instead, "How have I changed between these relationships?" You will always attract what you resonate into the world. If you feel victimized by the men in your past, not seeing what you have done to enable and encourage this undesirable situation, you will continue to attract similar situations until you are able to step into your true self as the creator of your life.

"Love like you have never been hurt before" is not only good advice once in a relationship, but it is even better advice for attracting a nurturing and loving relationship into your life. This kind of love takes courage and strength. It takes a trust in men, but more importantly in yourself. If you can trust that you are capable of handling whatever fate throws at you and are ready to accept the ups and downs of a true intimate relationship, only then are you truly ready for the kind of love you dream of.

People who had traumatic and abusive childhoods or who have never been truly cared for by anyone may not have learned what love feels like, and therefore, might not be unable to move toward true love. They may have linked the abuse with love because that is the only kind of attention they got. Even abusive attention is better than no attention, they figure. People like this need to learn what love feels like first to be successful in the quest for love. However, this is beyond the scope of this book, and I would encourage these people to reach out to me directly at my website, www.sukisohn.com.

Becoming Magnetic

While electricity is an outwardly expanding force and thus considered masculine, the magnetic is considered a feminine force. In order to create magnetic force, there must be polarity. Polarity is the state of having two opposite or contradictory tendencies or aspects.

As you can see with a simple magnet experiment, two poles of the same kind repel each other, while two opposite poles are instantly drawn to each other. When passion fizzles, it is usually because polarities have been diminished between the sexes. When a man stops feeling like a man, he will withdraw his energy and attention. When you stop feeling like a woman around your lover, very likely you will reject him or withdraw yourself by shutting down emotionally.

According to Kabbalists and Taoists, men are of the Yang or positive pole, which simply means it is the active and expansive pole. Women are, on the other hand, the magnetic and receptive pole. There is no judgement of what is good or better. It simply is. If a man is not allowed or able to express his essence of being the giving force and a woman, her essence of the being the receiver, the polarities diminish and attraction falters. Are you able to identify traits in yourself that disallow a man to feel that he is providing, protecting, and pining for you?

The Lure of the Chase

Among mammals in the animal kingdom, the males always pursue the female. What humans define as beauty is actually an indication of health to the subconscious mind – symmetry of face, clear complexion, lustrous hair, and specific body proportions that signal fertility. A mate who meets these biological standards externally is considered attractive and is more often pursued by men. In return, women size up the potential of their suitors with similar standards to ensure the best possible genetics for offspring.

Men processing larger testosterone are the active agents in the game of mating, while the females are looking towards long-term connection for rearing their young. On a biological level, little has changed since the advent of feminism. A woman capable of being "passive" yet open, and alluring is likely to attract more men, as this indicates a confidence in their attributes to attract a male. Overly aggressive pursuit by a woman would not be attractive to most men because it emasculates them.

The pursuit is an indication that a man finds you attractive and worthy, and further fuels his desire for connection and coital bliss. It is the confidence of a woman who knows herself worthy of pursuit that's truly attractive. He finds joy and thrill in the chase of a worthy woman. Why not sit back and enjoy the game instead of giving up your keys to the kingdom too quickly? Never trust what a man says, especially during this phase of courting. Watch what he does. Does he walk his talk? Grant him the thrill of chasing you, while you take this time to size up his suitability as a long-term partner.

Boundaries are Sexy

For men who are biologically engineered to pursue a mate, boundaries of women are incredibly sexy. Boundaries pose an immediate challenge which makes the pursuit more interesting for a confident and worthy suitor. Also, a woman with boundaries demonstrate self-esteem which make her more desirable. As the relationship matures, having healthy boundaries will save you from a co-dependent or worse an abusive relationship

Boardroom to Bedroom

If you are a woman working in a male-dominated field or in a managerial position, you may find that you have trouble transitioning from the boardroom to the bedroom. Your body language and tone may take on an assertive and practical manner at work, and you may be unconsciously bringing this to your date, and possibly into the bedroom.

I hear clients like this lament that they don't feel feminine anymore. If you are a single woman, the primary breadwinner for you children, and haven't had a date in a while, it's not surprising you find yourself disconnected from the mannerisms of feminine romantic love. Needless to say, no lover wants to be spoken to like a staff member or colleague.

I recommend to my clients to always take time to shake off the workday so they can transition into their personal lives. You could take a scented warm bath, apply a fresh coat or different shade of lipstick and another piece of jewelry, or change clothes into something less professional. The key is to be mindful of this transition. Please review Chapter 6: Navigate and Nourish Your Body for more suggestions on reclaiming femininity.

Myth of Mr. Right

If you are still holding on to a list of qualifications for Mr. Right, then you are doing yourself a major disservice. These kinds of lists are a product of your head brain – logic and reason. I guarantee you that a choice made by your head brain alone, without the heart and gut brains' blessings, will inevitably lead to an unfulfilling and limited relationship. The conscious mind is limited by its own experience. Laura, for instance, would never been able to accept Tony into her life without a willingness to follow her heart and gut. So throw out your mental Mr. Right check list and take a chance on what the universe has in store for you.

The Need for Discernment

Now that we got rid of our checklist for Mr. Right you might be thinking: What about discernment? Shouldn't there be some criteria in selecting our partners?

There is a fine line between discernment and distrust. When you are cautious and withdrawn meeting someone for the first time, what are the thoughts that go through your mind? "Is he trustworthy?", "Is he going to hurt me?", "Does he find me attractive enough?", "Will he stick around, or will he leave me like the other men in my life?" What kind of signals do you think you would be unconsciously emitting with these kinds of thoughts? On the contrary, how would things be different if you were truly curious and genuinely interested in the person in front of you instead of counting the reasons why you need to be protect yourself? Mr. Right checklists and even the caution you think is discernment may be attracting to you exactly what you fear.

Vanity vs. Self-Respect

There is a fine line between vanity and self-respect. A woman who takes care of herself and has lots of self-love and appreciation for her body will be less concerned about how she is perceived by others than those driven by vanity. Vanity requires validation by others, self-respect needs validation from nobody. Vanity gives your power away to another. The external result may be the same, but the internal effect will be worlds apart. One will lead to a positive cycle of gratitude and appreciation for one's body, while the other will lead to constant negative self-talk, chasing an unachievable ideal of beauty.

Love at First Sight?

I truly believe that, for a few lucky people, love at first sight does exist. But many factors have to come together for this to happen.

First, the body must recognize a good complimentary match driving the biological need for closeness, the heart must be open and ready for commitment, and the head must put aside logic and reason and surrender to the magic of it all. However, no matter how blissful and strong the attraction seems at first, love is like a plant that needs to be nurtured continually.

Sometimes lust or a remembrance of a past life connection is mistaken for love at first sight. You may be drawn to somebody purely driven by your body recognizing a suitable sperm donor. Alternatively, you may feel a strong connection because of a familiarity your soul recognizes.

How would you recognize true love vs. these other situations? Love is not conditional. It wants nothing in return. Being able to share your love feels like a gift to yourself. Your desire is not only for the pleasure of the company of your lover, but for the genuine happiness of your beloved, whether that is with or without you.

Meeting Your Inner Lover

As I had mentioned earlier, I went on a Vision Quest into the wilderness of Arizona with a burning desire to find deeper wisdom to guide myself and others. I didn't know what to expect, and what I came up away with was certainly not what I imagined it to be.

One completely unexpected encounter was meeting my inner lover. In a delirious trance state, I heard a whisper in my ear, "My beloved… take your clothes off and make love to me." I obeyed without resistance and made love to my inner lover stark naked in the wild, under the sun. I call my inner lover my Dark King, because he somehow encompassed all of masculinity

– including the negative traits of masculinity like violence and aggression that I had attributed to men. During this union with my inner beloved, I realized that what I had rejected in men was also *in me*, and that by accepting this, I was able to truly forgive the men that had hurt and betrayed me in the past.

I can now call upon my Dark King any time. As I stare at myself reflected in a mirror, I can see myself through the eyes of my inner lover – full of desire and passion. As Rumi said, our lovers are within us all along. Finally acquainted with my inner lover, I was able to truly fall madly and passionately in love with myself.

Artists call this inner lover their muse. It is that entity within us that drives us towards greater self-love, passion, and creativity in life. Your inner lover usually is represented as the opposite sex, but not always. Your relationship with this inner lover determines your level of passion and love for yourself.

I led Maria, the voluptuous seductress who unconsciously believed men to be mere toys for her physical pleasure, through an encounter with her inner lover. In her vision, the inner lover was a magnificent black bird. When she emerged from the session, she was weeping profusely and said that she never felt so loved and desired. She never felt a love and longing so strong. Shortly after this session, Maria was able to open her heart to a man to whom she is now engaged to be married.

Not knowing that your true lover is within, you may seek and project the desire for your inner lover onto men. But no man can ever live up to your inner lover. A faint shadow of your relationship with your inner lover is what gets reflected onto a romantic love with a man. In relating to a man, accept him for who he is and don't project your inner lover onto him. This will only lead to disappointment, because you are asking him to fill a hole that only you can fill with your inner lover.

Even more so than biological factors, being sexy and attractive comes from a state of mind and attitude that radiates from within. As Sophia Lauren said, "Nothing makes a woman more beautiful than the belief that she is beautiful." Developing a strong relationship with your inner lover is a surefire way to be in this state of mind.

In the Buddhist sutra called the Raja, there is a story of powerful King Pasenadi who asks his beloved queen Mallika who the dearest person to her in the world is. He of course expects the answer to be himself. But the wise queen answers that it is she herself who is most dear to her. King Pasenadi realizes that the same is true for him. The king and queen seek the Buddha about this, and he confirms the truth of their discovery with this teaching:

> *I visited all quarters with my mind nor found I any*
> *dearer than myself; Self is likewise to every other dear;*
> *who loves himself may never harm another.*

Buddha teaches that true compassion and love ultimately comes from a deep love for the self.

Divine Timing

I met my husband at a moving meditation class. We were friends for a few years before we started dating. Had we started dating when we first met, I am sure it would not have lasted. We both needed to go through our own personal transformations for us to be ready for each other. I was a single mother for nearly six years before we finally got together. At times, I wondered if I would ever find love again, let alone be remarried. Trusting the process was difficult. Unfortunately, if a healthy and fulfilling relationship is what you are looking for, the process of self-discovery and transformation is a pre-requisite. Do your own work and trust in the divine timing.

Where and How to Meet a Man

Many women want to know where and how to meet men. Well … first of all, stop saying you're looking when you really aren't. Eligible men are everywhere. Stop desperately looking for a man, hoping that he will complete your life somehow. You just need to understand what might be blocking you from meeting and attracting them to you. So the question isn't where and how do I meet men, but rather, how am I blocking myself from attracting men into my life?

You might be unconsciously avoiding meeting new people and refusing to be in social situations. Once bitten, twice shy, as the saying goes. It really is not unusual for women to feel socially awkward and perhaps even painfully shy. For single moms who have so much to juggle, pursuing social activities may even seem unrealistic. But that is simply your belief. Freeing yourself from fear of rejection and hurt is your first step. If you lack the courage to take another chance on love or simply aren't ready, an army of possible suitors could be knocking down your door and they will be invisible to you.

Perhaps you are looking with such desperation that you suck the energy out of anyone you meet. How do you feel about your own company? If you can't stand being in your own company, why should anyone else? A healthy relationship requires two whole people. Actively pursue your own life and interests. Become a person who has a lot to bring to the table.

Modern Love

If it's been a while since you have been dating, you will find a very a different technological landscape. There are many websites and mobile apps that give you an unlimited number of potential suitors. The resistance you may feel in putting yourself in social situations may also translate into this space. I had several clients meet their husbands using these tools, so I do believe it is a great place to meet people. However, these tools are getting more and more impersonal. As one client described it, "Before, it was all lengthy profiles and revealing charming details about yourself, followed by a polite exchange of get-to-know-you-banter emails and arrangements to meet for coffee. Now, it is a lot of pictures and swiping right, followed by some text messages if you're lucky." She found the whole process demoralizing and futile, yet she felt like it seemed to be the only place she could meet people.

Online dating apps allow people to cast the net wider, and as such, you will likely face more rejections. It's like going on a lot of auditions or sending your resume out to many different companies: With more auditions and applications filled, there will also likely be more rejections. Also, unlike the old-school way of dating, where you were able to gauge the other person's interest before making a move, now you are staring at a doctored profile picture with no other biological or behavioral cues to go by. You need to approach the whole process with light-heartedness and humor. Online or old school, energetic principles of attraction do not change.

Dealing with Rejection

Human experience of rejection goes back to our ancient roots. Scientists claim that the emotional and physical pain we experience in rejection was an early warning system (Winch, *Emotional First Aid*). During our ancestral hunter-gatherer times, social ostracism equated death. Without the numbers and the shelter your tribe provided, humans were a fragile species with no natural biological defense mechanism against predators. Thus, pain of rejection was built into our DNA to increase our chance of survival by falling in line with the tribe. On a physiological level, rejection triggers the same brain pathways that are activated when we experience physical pain. Scientists also found that the brain releases natural painkillers, or opioids, in response to social pain identical to that released in the face of physical pain. Unlike our ancestral tribal times, rejection does not equal ostracism or death. Though sometimes it feels like it.

Suffering in life is inevitable. I do not intend to convey a negative worldview, but rather, propose a pragmatic perspective that deals with the world as it is. The degree to which we suffer is determined by two things. The first is our level of resistance to the incident, and the second is our degree of attachment to a certain outcome. Our brain is wired to avoid pain, and thus will use all of its tools at hand to help us move away from pain. Unfortunately, often it is this very resistance that keeps us stuck in the state of suffering. Sometimes, the fastest way to overcome something is through it. Fully accepting your emotional state instead of trying to rationalize the cause of it is the fastest way to release the pain. When you first feel the sting of rejection, immediately use the Managing Emotional Flood Tool presented in Chapter 4 to fully accept the discomfort you are facing, but give yourself a different perspective of it. When we are in a strong emotional state, we tend to completely identify with it, feeling that it is all there is. You have emotions. You are not the emotion itself. Emotions are like the weather. It changes all the time. During times of grief, however, it feels like it will never end – but one thing that will never change is change itself.

A strong attachment to a desired outcome keeps us stuck in the pain of rejection. It is natural for humans to want to be liked. This goes back to our ancestral tribal history and fear of ostracism. You are bound to meet people who you are not compatible with, yet whether you were attracted to your date or not, you will most likely want to feel desirable. But what would it feel like if you were okay whatever the outcome may be? What if you could approach every encounter with curiosity instead of an attachment to the outcome of being seen as desirable? Your ability to face rejection with resilience, and even a sense of humor and grace, will depend on your level of self-esteem. High self-worth allows you to be less attached to specific outcomes. When you are narrowly focused on a specific outcome, you constrict your heart and your very being into a small and shriveled up version of yourself. Here is a simple exercise to expand your being and release attachment to outcomes.

EXERCISE: Expanding Heart

It is the sense of separation and isolation we feel from others that keeps us bitter and in a passive and powerless victim mentality. The outcome-obsessed, in-resistance version of you will only persist if you choose it. The following exercise allows you to release attachments, tension, and feel a oneness with your surroundings. This larger and elevated version of you is your true self, and this version of you is truly beautiful and magnetic.

1. Take a comfortable seat with your back straight. Take a few deep breaths.
2. Place your hands on your heart and bring your focus to your heart.

3. Now picture someone you love dearly, a special someone or something you think of that brings a smile to your face and warms your heart.

4. Breathe naturally and pay attention to the sensation you feel in your heart. Focusing on your beloved subject, continue to deepen the feeling of love in your heart. Feel the physical sensation of love in your heart.

5. When you feel a strong stirring and connection to your heart, very slowly expand your hands out, feeling that sensation travel through your arms. As you expand the warm sensation of love from you heart to arms, imagine this love as a ball of light that grows and expands to envelop your whole body.

6. Imagine that light further expanding, and now bring into that light people from the past that have hurt you or disappointed you. Shower them with the light of your love.

7. Watch how these people transform in your light.

8. If you feel yourself contract, connect back to the original sensation of love in your heart.

9. If you still feel contracted, connect to Mother Earth through the soles of your feet, and by beaming your light to her to ask her to support you in expanding your heart. Next, beam a light from the top of your head to the sky and into the cosmos. With this beam of light, ask Father Sky to infuse you with the power to open your heart. Feel Mother Earth and Father Sky sending you their love and energy.

10. Notice how your heart and body feels. Notice how you feel towards those people that have hurt you in the past.
11. When you feel calm, gently place your hands on your thighs and open your eyes.
12. Journal about what came up for you during the exercise.

PART III

Relating to Your Environment

CHAPTER 9

Illuminate Your Guilt

"Guilt is a useless feeling.
It's never enough to make you change direction--
only enough to make you useless"
-DANIEL NAYERI

G uilt is not only a useless emotion, it often masks your true fears and gives you an excuse for inaction. It is critical to see the true identity of your guilt to break free of the trappings of being undeserving and endless procrastination.

Paula was a single mom with a teenage son. She got divorced when her son was a toddler and she never looked back. She was content with her job and her son was the "man" in her life. She devoted her life to raising him. She felt guilty about the time she spent away from her son at work, so she took a job with limited growth prospects but which allowed for flexibility. Now that her son is a teenager and about to go off to college, she is mortified about the prospect of being alone. Encouraged by her son, she started to look on dating sites, but feels completely like a fish out of water in the game of romance.

It is truly one of the most unfortunate scenarios when a woman believes she needs to sacrifice her own life for that of her children. Although our children come through us, they are human beings with their own life paths to follow. It is not uncommon to see moms (single or married) in a relationship bound by guilt with their children. Initially, the mother feels guilty for not being enough for their children. For a working mom, she feels guilty for not being physically there for her children, while some stay-at-home moms often feel guilty for not pursuing a life of their own. Later in life, when the children start asserting their independence as young adults, I see mothers use guilt to manipulate and control their children.

Khalil Gibran speaks beautifully of parenting:

You are the bows from which your children as living arrows are sent forth.

The archer sees the mark upon the path of the infinite,

and He bends you with His might that His arrows may
go swift and far.

Let your bending in the archer's hand be for gladness.

A woman without "a room of her own" will not be able to let go of her children with gladness, which is truly tragic for both mother and child. If you would like your children to spread their wings and fly to meet their potential, model this for your children in your own life.

The truth behind a woman who believes that she must sacrifice her own life to be a good mother is that she is using her guilt as an excuse to avoid the things she fears. A mother who models a life confined by fears will convey the same message to her daughters and sons. Various epigenetic studies show our choices affect our DNA, and this change can be carried down as far as 14 generations (Lipton, *Biology of Beliefs*).

They say it takes a village to raise a child, and in ancient times the tribe collectively looked after the children. Traditional indigenous tribal practices are worthwhile, especially in light of the drastic rise of ADHD, anxiety disorders, depression, teen suicides, and obesity in the last fifty years. Psychologist Peter Gray links the decline in communal play to the rise in lost opportunities to make friends, learn self-control, develop intrinsic motivation, and other basic developmental functions as the key factor in the rise of psychopathologies in children. Also, research in Western societies finds that children of single parent families greatly benefit from having other adults around, even when it is someone they meet only weekly such as a sports or music teacher (Gray, *Free to Learn*).

Bring a light to your guilt and see it for what it truly is. Stop with the martyrdom. Do yourself, your lover, and your children a favor and face your fears.

CHAPTER 10

Create a Supportive Environment

Your environment, which is made up of the community and space you live in, has a powerful influence over your life. In this chapter, we will discuss how to create an environment that is supportive of your well-being and your desire for love.

Friends & Community

Birds of a feather flock together. Your friends and community influence the choices you make and ultimately your life. Do you surround yourself with friends that commiserate the woes of life and may unconsciously have a vested interest in keeping you from having the kind life you want?

I recall one evening after having dinner with my friend Leah, who was going through marital trouble, being particularly unpleasant towards my husband. My ever-so-intuitive husband asked who I had dinner with, and when I told him, he understood why I was being so short with him. My friend was angry and bitter towards her husband and by extension all men. When I came home I realized I was unconsciously bringing Leah's story into mine. This is the Law of Congruity. The frequencies you surround yourself with affect your own frequency. Humans, being pack animals, gravitate towards similar patterns whether they are good or bad for us.

Shifts in yourself will inevitably result in some friends falling away and that's okay. The books you read (i.e. information you take in) and the company you keep influences you in more ways than you are conscious of. Kabbalists had advised to be careful of your choices in information and friends you surround yourself with, as the Law of Congruency dictates you will be shaped by them.

Feng Shui for Promoting Love

Ancient traditions understood that the space we inhabit has a strong influence on our emotional and physical well-being. More recently, studies have shown that patients who stay in hospital rooms with a view towards trees and nature have a faster recovery rate (Ulrich, "View Through a Window May Influence Recovery from Surgery"). Major cathedrals and temples were always built on energetic centers, also known as lei lines. Feng Shui is a comprehensive codification of the many tools to create a living environment that supports the well-being of its inhabitants.

Feng Shui masters believe that our living environment reflects our inner energy state and vice versa. When we shift our internal state, it is reflected in our living spaces. For example, when you get depressed, I bet you find your living space messy and neglected. To remedy this, we can start by shifting our inner state: A more orderly environment will follow. Feng Shui masters know that you can also shift your inner energy state by shifting your environment. Many find it is easier to shift something external than to transform your inner state. However, the very act of making this shift in your environment with the focused intention starts sending out your wishes to the universe.

Here are some specific examples on how to promote more romance and passion in your life with Feng Shui principles.

The Bagua and the Relationship Corner

The Bagua is used in Taoist cosmology to represent the fundamental principles of reality and energies of the world, seen as a range of eight interrelated concepts around the central point of earth. The Bagua can be superimposed on your living space to provide an understanding of the energy held in the different parts of the space. We will speak in more detail about the relationship and love corner of the Bagua.

Standing at your front door facing inwards, the farthest right corner of the room holds the energy of love and relationships.

Take a look at what is going on in this part of your room. What objects do you have in this part of your room? If you are looking to enhance your chances of a romantic relationship, I recommend that you make sure this corner is well clean and orderly.

Place a pair of objects in this corner to represent partnership. It is important that the objects are similar in size and shape. These two objects represent you and your lover. Picking two objects that are not identical yet similar in mass is a metaphor to achieve an equal partnership, instead of an unbalanced relationship where one person dominates the other. Also, when you place these objects make sure to "charge" them with your intention and a blessing, and visualize your desired outcome to a point where you can feel it in your body.

Wealth & Prosperity	Fame & Recognition	Love & Relationships
Family & Community	Health	Children & Future
Wisdom & Self Cultivation	Career & Opportunities	Mentors & Benefactors

Align this side with the Main Entrance to Your Room

I once worked with a client who had a large painting of a single female figure in her bedroom. She also always slept in the middle of her king-sized bed. Though she consciously wanted to attract a relationship, her habits and living space were not supporting her desires. Making subtle shifts such as replacing the single female painting to one of a pair of swans and making room for a future lover in her bed allowed her to open up to inviting a new love into her life.

The use of color is also an important element of Feng Shui and is used across many cultures to this date to bring prosperity and healing to the mind and body. Colors that promote passion, love, and romance are red, pink, and peach tones. Take a look at your bedroom. What colors dominate your room? Your element will most likely be influencing your preference in colors. Being of strong metal element, my bedroom was dominated in gray and white. In order to make sure my relationship was not lacking in passion, I added artwork and a throw that had strong red accents. Again make sure your intentions are clear when you place your color adjustments to program it with your intention.

You can, of course, use various colors to bring balance or bring in new qualities to your environment. For example, if you need more stability and calm in your life, you may choose to use beige and green tones.

Element	Preferred Colors	Qualities
Fire	Red, Pink, Peach	Passion, Romance
Earth	Beige, Brown, Yellow	Stability
Water	Black, Indigo	Wisdom, Intuition
Air	Light Blue, Turquoise	Joy, Levity
Metal	White, Gray	Purity, Order
Wood	Green	Growth, Healing

CHAPTER 11

The Curve Balls

J ust when we think we've figured out a few things, life tends to throw curve balls at us, testing if we have indeed matured and learned the lessons each challenge brings to our life. In this book, I have attempted to provide a series of principles and exercises for attracting and nurturing romantic love. In this chapter, I present a few possible obstacles in implementing these principles and recommendations to overcome them.

Managing Emotions

When dealing with life challenges, we are sometimes flooded with emotions that paralyze us. Our autonomic nervous systems respond to crises with three possible outcomes – fight, flight, or freeze.

Fight is usually accompanied with anger and a surge of energy, and when channeled correctly, it can be a powerful fuel for positive change. Using the exercise introduced in Chapter 4, *Managing the Emotional Flood*, could be a useful tool to master these strong emotions instead of being swept up by them. Emotions are energy in motion. Instead of being controlled by them, learn to use the energy created by strong emotions proactively and productively.

Flight, or in its more subtle form avoidance, is a tricky one to recognize. The brain is genius at rationalizing reasons to avoid what it perceives as pain or a threat. The rationale is sound and sensible. Hiding behind practicality, we avoid the changes we need to make in order to let go and move forward. This is when you need help to keep you honest and accountable. It is times like this that working with a coach is invaluable in helping you identify your blind spots and keep you committed to your growth.

Freeze is challenging to move through. In this mode, we become stuck in old patterns and do not have momentum to move forward. In this case, the best tool is compassion and gentleness. When we get stuck in a downward spiral, we tend to have thoughts that are self-critical and judgmental. When you are in this rut, do something nice for yourself. Take a warm bath, go for a walk, dance, listen to calming music – whatever makes you happy. Another good exercise is writing a letter to yourself. Imagine your best friend was in a similar rut and write a letter to her. Then read the letter to yourself out loud. Compassion is the most powerful tool to unwind any tension and blockage.

Power of Choice

You will falter and perhaps even talk yourself into giving up. Chose to grow, transform, and love every day. The power of choice is a concept that eludes many. When you truly chose something, your brain will find a way to narrow the gap between your choice and your current reality. Also, when the power of choice is fully understood and engaged it creates a sincerity in you that not only affects your every day behaviour, it creates a resonance into the Universe. And the Universe without doubt responds to sincerity.

Importance of Consistent Practice

The recommendations in this book will only be helpful if you apply them. I was once told the effects of knowledge by a sage Tibetan lama. He told me that at tanneries in Tibet, artisans rub butter on the skins to the soften the leather. This is like practice – constantly applying the knowledge acquired in life to soften edges of the mind allowing for supple adaptability to life's challenges. Artisans also store the butter in the skins, but when left too long, the skins harden like rocks and the butter and skin both become unusable. Knowledge acquired but unused, hardens the mind with pride and arrogance. You think you may know something because you read it and intellectually understood it, but until you put it into practice, the knowledge you acquired will only harden your mind against true wisdom.

More Resources

Even with the best of intentions and utmost sincerity, we are sometimes unable to see our blind spots. We may be in deep denial of our shortcomings, or sometimes certain experiences are too painful to revisit. Also, though we know what is best for us, sometimes it is difficult to get out of our habitual thought patterns and behavior. The inner resistance to change may be too great to overcome. I have introduced supplementary material to the book at www.sukisohn.com/resources that could be of further assistance. Of course, I am also happy to personally help you on your journey should you need it.

CHAPTER 12

Epilogue

We have explored the eight basic principles of the MAGNETIC Process to attract and nurture the romantic relationship of your dreams. Those principles were:

1. **M**ind your element to know what makes you attractive and avoid common relationship pitfalls for your type
2. **A**cknowledge and release the ghosts of your past
3. **G**reet and transform your demons into your allies
4. **N**avigate and nourish your body
5. **E**dify yourself on how men are different and elucidate yourself with compassion and clarity

6. **T**empt and tease your way into his heart by understanding the forces of attraction
7. **I**lluminate your guilt to understand its true identity
8. **C**reate a supportive environment

To love is to be vulnerable, yet is also the source of infinite strength. Love is a journey fraught with tests and trials for the soul, yet it is also the grounds from which courage and maturity springs. As an intuitive healer, I know without doubt that love and compassion are the source of a healer's ability to mend a broken heart and spirit.

Treat and talk to yourself the way you want to be treated and talked to. Be the kind of lover you want in your life to yourself before searching for one elsewhere, as the confidence, openness, and compassion you feel for yourself will magnetize the lover of your dreams.

Your ability to love another will start from your ability to love and respect yourself. Without knowing what it feels like to be truly, deeply, and unconditionally loved, resonating and attracting that kind of relationship will be difficult if not impossible. Our lovers are within us all along, and our life partners are simply a reflection of our own level of love and respect within. Those lucky enough to have enlightened and unconditionally loving parents may have experienced it as a child. But for many others, you may be on a lifelong journey to understand what love is and what it feels like. Love is, after all, one of life's greatest mysteries.

Here I would like to leave you with a prayer and blessing from the Lakota Indian tribes:

> *Great Mystery,*
> *teach me how to trust*
> *my heart,*
> *my mind,*
> *my intuition,*
> *my inner knowing,*
> *the senses of my body,*
> *the blessings of my spirit.*
> *Teach me to trust these things*
> *so that I may enter*
> *my Sacred Space and*
> *Love beyond my fear and thus*
> *Walk in Balance with*
> *the passing of each glorious Sun.*

SHARE YOUR STORY

I would love to hear from you on how what I have shared has impacted your romantic relationships. Please e-mail me at contact@sukisohn.com with your stories.

REFERENCES & RESOURCES

Chapter 2
Nørretranders, Tor. The User Illusion: Cutting Consciousness Down to Size. Penguin Books, 1999.

Chapter 4
Bennett, Jay. "The Double-Slit Experiment That Blew Open Quantum Mechanics." Popular Mechanics. July 28, 2016. <http://www.popularmechanics.com/science/a22094/video-explainer-double-slit-experiment/>

Weizmann Institute of Science. "Quantum Theory Demonstrated: Observation Affects Reality." ScienceDaily. ScienceDaily, 27 February 1998. <www.sciencedaily.com/releases/1998/02/980227055013.htm>

Australian National University. "Experiment confirms quantum theory weirdness." ScienceDaily. ScienceDaily, 27 May 2015. <www.sciencedaily.com/releases/2015/05/150527103110.htm>.

Chapter 5

Nørretranders, Tor. The User Illusion: Cutting Consciousness Down to Size. Penguin Books, 1999.

Lipton, Bruce. The Biology of Belief 10th Anniversary Edition: Unleashing the Power of Consciousness, Matter & Miracles. Hay House; 10th Anniversary edition. October 13, 2015.

Hawkins, David R. Power vs. force: the hidden determinants of human behavior. Carlsbad, CA: Hay House, Inc., 2014.

Soosalu, Grant. mBraining: Using your multiple brains to do cool stuff. CreateSpace Independent Publishing Platform, 2012.

Hanson, Rick. Buddha's Brain: The Practical Neuroscience of Happiness, Love, and Wisdom. New Harbinger Publications; 1st edition. 2009.

Chapter 6:

Nørretranders, Tor. The User Illusion: Cutting Consciousness Down to Size. Penguin Books, 1999.

Soosalu, Grant. mBraining: Using your multiple brains to do cool stuff. CreateSpace Independent Publishing Platform, 2012.

Levine, Peter. Waking the Tiger: Healing Trauma. North Atlantic Books; 1 edition. July 7, 1997.

McCraty, Rollin, Ph.D., Science of the Heart: Exploring the Role of the Heart in Human Performance Volume 2, Heart Math Institute Research, 2015.

Chapter 7:
Jantz, Gregory, Ph.D., "Brain Differences Between Genders," www.psychologytoday.com, February 27, 2014.

University of California, Irvine. "Intelligence in Men and Women Is a Gray and White Matter." ScienceDaily. 22 January 2005. www.sciencedaily.com/releases/2005/01/050121100142.htm

Chapter 8:
Sensiper, Sylvia, Dr. "The Biology of Attraction." www.monticelloinstitute.com

Boltzman, Ludwig. "Study Finds Signs of Elusive Pheromones in Human", NY Times, March 12, 1998.

Ryan, Michael J. "Sexual Selection, Receiver Biases, and the Evolution of Sex Differences." Science Magazine, Vol. 281, September 25, 1998.

Chapter 9
Winch, Guy. *Emotional First Aid: Practical Strategies for Treating Failure, Rejection, Guilt, and Other Everyday Psychological Injures.* Hudson Street Press, 2013.

Gray, Peter. Free to Learn: *Why Unleashing the Instinct to Play Will Make Our Children Happier, More Self-Reliant, and Better Students for Life*. Basic Books; 1 edition (March 5, 2013)

Chapter 10
Diamond, Jared. The World Until Yesterday. Viking Press; 1st edition. 2012.

Ulrich, Roger S. "View through a window may influence recovery from surgery." American Association for the Advancement of Science, 1984.

ACKNOWLEDGEMENTS

My first heartfelt gratitude goes to the numerous guides and teachers I have had during my journey to date, without whom my life would not be as rich and full of love as it is now. In particular, I am truly grateful for my Kabbalah teacher, Sarah Yardeni, who gently guided me towards my true calling as a guide and healer for others. When I first met her, I was a single mom working at a hedge fund making a six-figure paycheck but miserable inside. It was she who first opened my eyes to a different possibility not only for my career but my choices in love. Instead of insisting on Kabbalah being the only spiritual path like many teachers would have done, she encouraged me to study different paths to enrich my spiritual evolution.

I would also like to acknowledge my husband John O'Connor, who not only supported me through all my evolutions, dark and light, but also is always a constant source of inspiration for his commitment to our relationship, his own personal growth, and that of his clients. I am a lucky woman to have him as my life partner.

Thank you Angela Lauria for your firm, no BS guidance, and the fantastic team at Difference Press to make this book a reality not just an idea in my head.

To the Morgan James Publishing team: Special thanks to David Hancock, CEO & Founder for believing in me and my message. To my Author Relations Manager, Nia Baskfield, thanks for making the process seamless and easy. Many more thanks to everyone else, but especially Jim Howard, Bethany Marshall, and Nickcole Watkins.

Thank you to the Creator of all that is and the muses for choosing me as a channel to relate the messages in this book.

Lastly, my thanks go to you for being here and reading this book. My deepest joy comes from being able to soothe and guide those going through the dark night of their souls to the brilliance of their true self and the love that is present all around us.

ABOUT THE AUTHOR

Suki's journey into personal transformation started over a decade ago when her divorce and a string of failed relationships left her physically and emotionally depleted. As work stress mounted, she found herself with chronic back pain, insomnia, migraines, and depression that made her determined to regain her emotional and physical health. When MRIs, CT scans, and Western medical approaches did not provide satisfactory long-term answers or solutions, she looked to holistic mind-body-spirit approaches.

This led her to study many esoteric and spiritual paths. The exploration of these various paths led to her deep appreciation and fascination of the subtle energies that influence our daily lives. Through various timeless energy modalities, Suki now helps clients reclaim and optimize their emotional, mental, and physical well-being. We change our energy, we change our lives.

Another aspect of her work is developing inner resources through personal myths, stories, and metaphors. We unconsciously are exposed to, live by, and create intrinsic personalities and stories that run our lives. Used and cultivated mindfully, these personal archetypes can be powerful allies to strengthen our resilience to life's challenges. We change our stories, we change our lives.

Previously, Suki worked in finance and media with Fortune 100 companies such as the Walt Disney Company, News Corporation, Lehman Brothers, and Fortress Investment Group. She lives in Irvington, NY with her husband John O'Connor and two sons.

Website: www.sukisohn.com
Email: contact@sukisohn.com
Facebook: www.facebook.com/sukisohn.coach

THANK YOU!

To learn more about your unique qualities that make you irresistible and potential pitfalls that keep you stuck in heartbreak, go to https://www.sukisohn.com/quiz to find a complimentary assessment tool and video explanation and customized recommendations.

Morgan James
Speakers Group

We connect Morgan James published authors with live and online events and audiences who will benefit from their expertise.

Printed in the USA
CPSIA information can be obtained
at www.ICGtesting.com
JSHW082338140824
68134JS00020B/1738